BREAKFAST WITH LES AND BESS

A Comedy in Two Acts

by
Lee Kalcheim

SAMUEL FRENCH, INC.
45 WEST 25TH STREET   NEW YORK 10010
7623 SUNSET BOULEVARD HOLLYWOOD 90046
LONDON   TORONTO

**TO MY
MOTHER**

BREAKFAST WITH LES AND BESS was originally produced at the Hudson Guild Theater in New York City in October, 1982; under the direction of Barnet Kellman with the following cast:

Bess Christen Dischinger .... Holland Taylor
Les Dischinger....................... Keith Charles
Shelby Dischinger Everson.............. Amy Wright
Roger Everson......................... Tom Nolan
David Dischinger .... John Leonard
Nate Moody/Announcer............... Daniel Ziskie

BREAKFAST WITH LES AND BESS was subsequently produced on Broadway by Howard Burnett and David Jones at the Lambs Theater under the direction of Barnet Kellman with the following cast:

Bess Christen Dischinger .... Holland Taylor
Les Dischinger....................... Keith Charles
Shelby Dischinger Everson .... Kelle Kipp
Roger Everson .... Jeff McCracken
David Dischinger .... John Leonard
Nate Moody/Announcer.............. Daniel Ziskie

Set Design by Tschetter; Lighting Design by Ian Calderon; Costume Design by Timothy Dunleavy; Sound Design by Michael Jay; Production Stage Manager, Andrea Naier.

Opening Night: May 19, 1983

CHARACTER DESCRIPTIONS

BESS-   *a handsome woman, about 45. Smart, stylish New
        York career woman, thoroughly enjoys being a sophis-
        ticated member of the social set and a celebrity. Her
        career has always come first before all else. Public
        image very important to her, too important. So wrap-
        ped up in herself, she isn't usually sensitive or even a-
        ware of others. Never deliberately malicious just
        completely immersed in the things she feels are impor-
        tant. Hasn't admitted to herself that her life isn't
        everything she wants it to be.*

LES-   *attractive, charming man, late 40's. Sense of humor.
        Easy-going ex-baseball announcer and sports colum-
        nist, and he misses it. Hates his daily routine and the
        phony social obligations. Badly needs to change his life
        around and feel motivated again. Honestly believes
        that all of his and Bess' success has made them miser-
        able. Enjoys needling Bess but desparately wants
        them to be happy and in love again. Recognizes their
        problems and copes with them but is tired and fed up
        with merely coping.*

SHELBY- *cute, slighty dizzy, 20. Impulsive and kooky but in a
        sweet way. Badly needs attention and love but can
        pout and be defensive about her right to have it. Full of
        life and energy. Loves her parents and her brother even
        though it hasn't always been easy.*

DAVID- *rebellious, budding revolutionary typical of the 60's,
        also 20 years old. Would like to change the world over-
        night. Off-beat attitude toward life. A bit of a wise-
        cracking trouble-maker but really just a little mixed
        up. The lack of his parents' attention and approval has
        made him cynical. Not really a bad kid, just always
        seems to be in hot water because of his sometimes out-
        rageous behavior.*

CHARACTER DESCRIPTIONS
(continued)

ROGER-   *a handsome, beefy U.S. Naval Ensign about 25. Clean-cut, upright, practical Morman from Utah. Stable and secure. A healthy, normal American citizen totally unaccustomed to the New York "scene." At times, he is literally at sea as to how to handle his crazy new-found family.*

NATE-   *tall, lanky, 40's. Les' old broadcasting and drinking pal. Everybody's good-time buddy, ready for whatever comes along. Can definitely not handle his liquor, but takes great pains to hide it—unsuccessfully however.*

AUTHOR'S NOTE

One might call "Les and Bess" a light comedy. But I like to think there's more to it than meets the eye. It's a play about *change*. About how we get stuck in our lives..in our comforts..in our success, in our failure and can't get out. But Les, suddenly looks around at his deteriorating family, and at a world outside that is changing rapidly and asks himself... "Why can't I? Why can't we?" The one good thing he had in his life was his love for Bess. And there's been a microphone between them for ten years..keeping them from making contact. He wants that contact again. Les's determination to get that..and his strong feeling that deep down, Bess wants the love they once had too....is the drive behind the play. All of the comic moments will work, and indeed the play will be funnier if you keep in mind the central..call it..serious "spine," I've just described. Yes, this is a "crazy" family. They're fun to watch. But despite the fact they keep missing, and messing up ..there's a great deal of warmth. And we must see it in the quieter scenes. I like to think my plays work best when the rhythms are working. It may unfold slowly..then a moment of farce...then quiet...then more funny reparte'...rising to a payoff..then bang...a quiet moment. Les's long speech in Act Two is the best example of that. It starts as a funny drunken revel...and ends as the most deadly-serious..moving moment in the play. Make Les and Bess as *real* as possible and it will be funny *and* moving.

TIME

ACT I
Early morning (day one)

ACT II Scene 1
Early the following morning (day two)

ACT II Scene 2
Early the following morning (day three)

BREAKFAST WITH LES AND BESS

ACT ONE

Time: May, 1961.

*Set: The living room of an expensive New York City apartment. The
bi-level room is separated by a beige wrought-iron railing in
the center and two sets of steps, one stage right and one just to
the left of center. Each set of steps is only two steps down into
the main part of the room. The front door is upstage, just right
of center. There is an upstage center alcove with draped windows that overlook Central Park with a desk and chair in
front of them. The partially visible kitchen is through an up
left arch and two archways stage right lead to a hall with the
off-stage bedrooms and bathrooms. The room is furnished
tastefully. There is a built-in bookcase along the right wall
with a stereo unit. A mantled fireplace down right over which
the entire wall is covered with pictures of celebrities. Set
dressing includes several plants, autographed baseballs,
trophies, two Chinese vases on pedestals which flank the*

*kitchen arch, and a glass and chrome serving cart. There are
paintings, some small, valuable impressionists, lithos, etch-
ings and plaques. Downstage center is a large, comfortable
sofa with throw-pillows and a long credenza just above it.
Below it, a coffee table, and to the right of the sofa, an end
table. There is a large upholstered armchair just upstage of
the fireplace. Down left is a walnut cabinet which holds the
radio equipment and a dining table with chairs from which
LES and BESS do their early morning radio program.*

*In the dark (pre-curtain) we hear the sound of an early-morning
radio show's theme music, such as "Whistle While You
Work."* The pre-recorded voice of the HOST comes in over
the music.*

Host. Good morning, everybody. It's Monday, May
16th, 1961 and it's a beautiful May morning. I'm John
Corning here at WOR, Morning With Corning, and you'-
re obviously interested in what the day is going to be like
and it is going to be very pleasant indeed.

*(Lights up to reveal BESS CHRISTEN DISCHINGER, dressed
in a stunning robe and peignoir. She is taking the microphone
out of the cabinet downstage left and plugging it in to the console already on the dining table. The sound of the HOST'S
voice crossfades to the on-stage speaker in the cabinet and
continues under the dialogue.)*

*License to produce BREAKFAST WITH LES AND
BESS *does not include* the right to use this song.

HOST. Twenty minutes before eight o'clock. Just about time perhaps for you to get up. The day is going to be sunny and pleasant, a near perfect May day. We'll have a high today of probably somewhere near 70 degrees. The present reading here at WOR is 42 degrees with lots of nice bright sunshine, gentle winds and hardly a cloud in the sky. We're going to check the news in just a moment and then, of course, at eight o'clock it's time for "Breakfast With Les And Bess" ... *(continuing under dialogue)* Oh, and don't forget — today is the day of the ticker-tape parade honoring astronaut, Alan Shepard, and what a great day for a parade in New York. For more details...

BESS. *(Yells to the bedroom.)* Les! Les, it's twenty of. We go on the air in twenty-five minutes! *(She picks up the studio phone already set up on the table and speaks into it.)* Hi! All set. *(Leans toward microphone.)* Good morning, one two three four. *(into phone)* OK? What? OK. *(Hangs up. Looks to bedroom again and crosses upstage to front door.)* Les! Get up! *(Opens door, picks up newspapers from the hall, brings in the pile, slams door, turns again to bedroom. We should clearly be able to hear the HOST say, "Breakfast With Les And Bess," while she gets the papers, then:)* LES!!

LES. *(from off-right)* I'm up.

(Bess crosses down to the table and switches off the radio's monitor on the console.)

(The sound of the HOST'S voice is cut off. LES DISCHINGER

comes out of the bedroom thru the up right arch. He is still half asleep in wrinkled bathrobe, pajamas and slippers. He staggers slowly down-stage toward the sofa.)

LES. *(muttering)* I'm up. I'm up. I'm up. I'm up. I'm up. *(BESS has crossed to the coffee table. From the pile of newspapers she's holding she takes out the* Daily Variety *and the section of the* Daily News *which contains her column. She deposits them on the coffee table, puts the remaining pile of papers on the end-table at the right of the sofa and then crosses up to the desk. When LES reaches the sofa he collapses onto it with a final:)* I'm up. *(His head hits an Ensign's cap which he flings up above the sofa onto the floor, then he lies back, covering his head with a throw pillow to block out the light. BESS, who is getting her steno pad and a pencil at the desk, turns to see LES prone on the sofa.)*

BESS. *(at desk)* Les, please.

LES. Could you close the drapes?

BESS. It's nearly quarter of.

LES. Why don't you do the show alone. Talk deep for me.

BESS. *(Crosses down to center, sits on arm of sofa.)* It's a very special program this morning. Princess Grace is calling from Monaco.

LES. Do I have to dress up??

BESS. Come on! I want to make up a list of questions. I don't want you bumbling on the air.

LES. That's my style. Bumbling is my style!

BESS. Well, I don't think it will suit the Princess. *(Puts pad and pencil down on coffee table, crosses left to cabinet.)*

LES. *(mumbling)* The "Princess." She's an actress. She's

not even an actress. She's a bricklayer's daughter. Her whole country isn't as big as that park! Probably safer! *(He starts to nod off.)*

BESS. *(She shakes her head, goes to cabinet by table, to the automatic coffee maker and 2 pre-set cups .. pours some coffee ... takes him a cup.)* Here. *(Puts cup down on coffee table.)*

LES. *(Struggles to sit up, takes cup.)* You'd think after ten years, this would be easy. When I think about getting up early ... it seems *nice.* But doing it ... is so ... *(sips)* hard ... *(sips)* Like sex. *(sighs)* I guess that depends on who you're doing it with. *(sips)* I wonder if the same goes for getting up early.

BESS. *(Sits beside him, looking at her pad.)* I wrote up some questions last night.... Do you have anything you might want to ask Princess Grace?

LES. *(nods)* Yes!... What are *you* doing up???

BESS. Don't you have *anything* serious you'd like to ask her?

LES. Serious?

BESS. Yes!!

LES. No. *(BESS sighs, gets up, starts back up to desk, taking the "Daily Variety," her column and her pad with her.)* Oh ... Hey ... I got a new title for my book. You listening?

BESS. *(standing at R of desk with newspaper)* I'm just looking over my column — I can listen and look.

LES. OK. Listen to this title. "Take Two and Hit to Right." *(She shakes her head and looks at him.)* It's a baseball expression.

BESS. I got that.

LES. It's what the coach would tell a batter for the hit and run. Y'see ... the batter takes two pitches and on the third ... the man on first breaks for second and the batter hits the third pitch to right field .. behind the runner who then can go to third.

BESS. Why is that a good title for a book about crazy athletes?

LES. It's not about crazy athletes ... it's about "unconventional" athletes.

BESS. So?

LES. Well ... take two and hit to right ... it's a kind of conventional baseball expression ... and I thought there'd be some irony in having it be the title of a book about unconventional ... sports ... figures ... I guess not.

BESS. Why don't you write the book *first* ... and think of a title later.

LES. I *am* writing it. I've written a chapter and a half.

BESS. In five years? That's not writing. That's dawdling!

LES. If I had a title, the book would take off!

BESS. *Finish* the book. If it's a good book, the title won't matter. *(She puts down her column and starts looking through "Variety.")*

LES. OK!!!

(SHELBY enters from the bedrooms, thru DSR arch in her bathrobe.)

SHELBY. Hi!

LES. *(Leans toward her.)* Hi......

BESS. Where've *you* been???

SHELBY. In the bedroom. *(Leans down and kisses LES on the cheek.)*

BESS. *(Stands at the top of the C steps.)* I mean for the last two days? You said you were going to a party two nights ago.

SHELBY. Oh .... uh ....

LES. *(Picks up the "Herald Tribune" from the end-table.)* Must have been some party.

SHELBY. Yeah ... well uh ... it was kind of dull, really.

LES. How can you stay at a dull party for two days??

SHELBY. I was ... hoping it would get better.

BESS. Shelby, honey, we were worried. You could have at least called us and told us where you were.

SHELBY. Can't a person leave home for two days without all this worrying?

BESS. You're only twenty.

SHELBY. Alexander the Great was only twenty when he conquered Persia.

LES. But his folks knew where he was! *(Both LES and BESS are now engrossed in their respective newspapers, not paying any attention to SHELBY.)*

SHELBY. *(sighs)* OK ... I was gonna save it till after the show when you had some time ... but ... if you really want to know what I was doing ... well... *(She looks up to see LES, settled in couch with paper, open and BESS with her face now in "Variety." She stands a second, watching them read.)*

BESS. *(leaning against center railing)* Look at this. "Goldberg Leaves Warners For Metro..."

LES. "Rusk Leaves Paris For Moscow." I think Goldberg's got a better deal.

BESS. *(She smiles weakly, reads on.)* Sid Jarnoff had a three-picture deal at Fox. That jerk! He couldn't make a movie if his life depended on it.

LES. Looks like Kennedy's gonna meet Kruschev. *(SHELBY exits thru DSR arch.)* That should be fun. This fat Georgian peasant. And this Harvard upper-class Catholic ... Kruschev'll eat him up. *(Turns page.)*

BESS. Hummmm. Joan Crawford's in town. Plugging her new movie. She'll probably be the mystery guest on Sunday night's show. You know they hate me when I guess it so easily. But all you have to do is read the papers and you can *see* who's in town! *(She crosses up to desk for a pencil. Neither of them have noticed that SHELBY has left the room.)*

LES. Haile Selassie's in town. Gonna speak at the UN.

BESS. I doubt if he'd want to be a TV Mystery Guest.

LES. I'll bet no one ever asked him.

BESS. The general public doesn't know who he is!

LES. Sounds like the perfect mystery guest! *(He looks in the direction of where SHELBY was standing, shrugs, then continues to read.)*

BESS. *(Sighs, goes back to paper.)* Listen! *(reads)* Oh noooo! "CBS to drop talk shows." *(She walks slowly DS as she reads, sits next to him on sofa.)* "CBS radio's *At Home With The Hartley's* and *What's Cooking* will be dropped from the CBS schedule at the end of this month. Only Arthur Godfrey's afternoon show remains, CBS spokesman said. 'We are following the clear trend toward music programming.' It is evident that the high ratings of local "pop" music stations are tolling the deathknell for the once-popular radio talk show." *(She looks up at him.)* What do you *think?*

LES. Forget about Princess Grace. Let's play records!

BESS. Les, this is *serious.*

Les. It's not *that* serious.

Bess. Our show could be next. Our show could be dropped next!

Les. We've had a good run. What the hell! C'est la vie.

Bess. You don't mean that?

Les. Nothing lasts forever.

Bess. *(Rises, crosses left to table.)* You're full of brilliant cliche's this morning. Why don't you call the station and ask Steiner if something's up?

Les. He's not gonna *tell us* anything. When our show is dropped we'll read it in the trades like everyone else!

(Phone rings.)

Bess. I'll bet that's him now. That would be just like him. To cancel us ten minutes before we go on! *(Sits at the table.)* You better get it, I'm too upset to talk to him.

Les. *(Shrugs, reaches for the phone behind him on the credenza.)* Hello. Ohhhh Hello.

Bess. *(Rises, crosses in to sofa.)* Is it Steiner???

Les. *(Shakes, "no.")* Well it's nice to talk to you too! Is it beautiful there?

Bess. It's Princess Grace. Oh my God, it's Princess Grace! *(She runs up to the desk for her pad and runs back to the sofa.)*

Les. Yes ... I know ... Oh ... that's a shame.

Bess. Is it Princess Grace? Les, is it Princess Grace???

Les. NO! It's Mrs. Dalcimer!

Bess. Who???

LES. Mrs. Dalcimer. The couple who are renting the Connecticut house.

BESS. Oh. Yes.

LES. Their dog ate a piece of sculpture and she wants to know if it's valuable.

BESS. What piece?

LES. *(to phone)* What piece? *(Listens. To BESS.)* The head.

BESS. What piece of sculpture?

LES. *(to phone)* What piece of sculpture? *(Listens. To BESS.)* She thinks it was a woman, but she's not sure without the head. What? ... Oh ... yes ... she checked and she is sure.

BESS. *(Crosses left to table.)* It's the Haitian woman. Ohhh God. We should have put all those things away.

LES. Is it valuable?

BESS. Not terribly. It's just beautiful. *(Sits at table.)*

LES. *(into phone)* Don't worry, Mrs. Dalcimer. It's not valuable ... no no no. It *can't* be replaced. Don't feel badly. Yes it was beautiful. Your dog has good taste.... Well, that would be nice. Thanks. Bye. *(Hangs up. To BESS.)* They feel badly. They're going to get us a gift.

BESS. *(writing notes in her pad)* I can't wait to see that. We should never have rented the house.

LES. We never use it!

BESS. That's not the point. There are too many beautiful things in that house for it to be lived in!! *(He does an obvious take for her benefit. She checks watch.)* Ohhh ... look at the time. We have eight minutes ... I don't have nearly enough questions for Princess Grace.

LES. Ask her if she'd like to rent the Connecticut house.

BESS. I'm going to call the station. I'm just going to ask Steiner about that article in the trades. *(She crosses up to the phone on the desk and dials.)*

LES. He won't tell the truth. He's a producer!

(Phone rings. LES reaches for it.)

LES. *(into phone)* Hello. Hilga, where are you?

BESS. *(on other phone)* Bob ... it's Bess ... I read the trades this morning about the CBS talk shows ... I just wanted to find out if we're *(Turns US.)*

LES. You what??? Why?... Uhhhh Hilga ... Why don't you come in and talk to Mrs. Dischinger about this? Yes .. I .. but I really think you should do something like this in person. Hilga. Hilga. Hilga. *(BESS and LES hang up at the same time.)*

LES. *(Picks up his cup and crosses UL into kitchen.)* That was our maid.

BESS. *(Crosses down, sits at table.)* Where is she? She was supposed to be here an hour ago.

LES. She just quit.

BESS. *(Rises, steps to C, pacing.)* She quit? Why??

LES. Too many parties!

BESS. Too many parties?? Why ... we haven't had a party in two weeks...

LES. *(Crosses back in with small pastry box.)* We had one two nights ago.

BESS. That wasn't a party. That was just twenty for dinner.

LES. *(Sits on L side of table.)* Well, for her that was a party.

BESS. What does she expect for eighty-five dollars a week?!

LES. What did Steiner say?

BESS. *(Crosses into kitchen.)* She could have at least given us notice. What is it with help these days?

LES. You wanna know the truth? Help has never been any good. The Greeks had lousy help.

BESS. *(Returns to table with 2 linen napkins.)* It's not funny...

LES. It's all right. We'll get another maid. We'll have less parties. What *did Steiner say?*

BESS. Steiner assured me that the station has no plans whatsoever for cancelling our show.

LES. That's the kiss of death.

BESS. We're their number-one talk show.

LES. Double kiss. *(BESS starts to pace again in the center of the room. LES is munching on cookies from the pastry box and looking at the "Variety" on the table.)*

BESS. Well, just for insurance's sake ... we are going to keep ourselves on top. This Princess Grace interview is coming at a perfect time. A perfect time. I told him to be *sure* and listen this this morning. He's got a promo for it on the News... It's really got to be a fantastic interview.... We've got to keep the shows really up for the next few weeks. *(She crosses back to table. sits, makes notes in pad.)* I'll call Crawford's agent. Maybe we can grab her while she's in town.

LES. *(Rises, crosses back to sofa with coffee cup and sits.)* And Haile Selassie!

BESS. Les, this is important. I don't trust Steiner's assurances any more than you do ... but if we keep our audience, he's got to keep us. *(She rises and crosses to him.)*

LES. One question.

BESS. What?

LES. Do we have to keep him?

(The studio phone on the table buzzes and lights up.)

BESS. *(answering it)* Yes. Thank you. *(Hangs up.)* Five minutes. Now, I don't know exactly when Princess Grace is going to call. She said about eight-thirty. That'll give us a nice half hour with her. But, if she begs off, we'll read some letters from the refugee kids. Everybody likes those. *(She crosses up to desk.)* Oh, don't forget, there's a reception tonight for them.

LES. For who?

BESS. For the refugee children. At the Waldorf. And there's a private party latter at Manny Cherners. *(Crosses down to table with folders and clipboard.)*

LES. *(rises)* I can't go.

BESS. Why not?

LES. *(Exits thru DSR arch.)* I'm going to a fight in Philadelphia.

BESS. *(Crosses to USR arch.)* You're going to a fight in Philadelphia.

LES. *(Appears at USR arch.)* There's a kid fighting down there tonight. Dick Jessup saw him. Says he's *terrific. (Starts to exit.)*

BESS. Les, I....

LES. *(appears)* Jessup *knows* fighters. Says he's terrific. *And* I can buy a piece of him! *(Exits into bedroom, gets handkerchief.)*

BESS. *(sighs)* Oh, Les. All the things you've invested in were "terrific." The restaurant that folded. The Broadway play that closed on opening night, the.....

LES. *(Appears, wipes glasses, crosses DR.)* No, no, no, no. Dick says this kid is another Billy Conn! You remember Billy Conn. We saw the Conn-Lewis fight at the polo grounds in '41. Louis knocked him out in the 13th.

BESS. And this kid's another Billy Conn?!

LES. Conn was a great fighter. He almost beat Lewis. *(He sits in armchair.)*

BESS. *(Crosses down to him.)* Almost is not a good investment!

LES. If there's a kid around like Billy Conn, he's a good investment. You remember that fight? *(BESS shakes her head, crosses left to table, sits and looks thru her folders.)* It was terrific! Even *you* thought so. Remember, we went to that wild party afterwards up in Harlem. Billy Holiday sang. Oh Jesus ... was that a night. *(He looks at her, tenderly, and crosses in between sofa and coffee table.)* Hey ... why don't you and I go down to Philly tonight. We'll have dinner on the train, like old times. We'll see the fight ... go to the Golden Slipper Club, and stay over at the Bellvue. *(He kneels on the sofa, facing her.)*

BESS. I can't. We....

LES. We'll be back for the show. We'll get up early. *I'll* actually *get up early!* We'll take a limo back.... Come onnn...

BESS. We can't. We promised we'd go to the Refugee Reception. We're sponsers.

LES. *(He turns and strangles a sofa pillow.)* Those damn refugee kids. They *can't* need as much help as we give them!!!

(Phone rings.)

LES. *(Picks up phone on the credenza and sits on sofa.)* Hello. David ... Where are you? Are you at the same party your sister was at? You're where? Why? ... You what??? *(as he listens to the descriptions)* Oh, David... Oh, David... Oh, David...

BESS. Oh, David what?

LES. Well, that's good news.

BESS. What's good news?

LES. Well, that's not such good news.

BESS. Can you talk to him later? We're going on shortly.

LES. Just a minute. *(to BESS)* Our son's in jail.

BESS. Oh God, no.

LES. Oh God, yes.

BESS. What's he done now???

LES. Drove into Central Park Lake.

BESS. How could he do that?

LES. It was an accident. He was trying to impress some girl with his driving skills and...

BESS. No. How could he do that after the last accident? You forbade him to drive the car.

LES. He obviously disobeyed me.

BESS. You took his car keys. Where did he get keys?

LES. Does that matter now??? He's in jail. We have to get him out!

BESS. *(Rises, crosses to sofa.)* Were there any reporters around? Did anyone get any pictures?

LES. Is that really important?

BESS. Yes, it's important! Any bad publicity is just what

the station needs to try to get us off the air. We don't need this now. *(up to the "Heavens")* We don't need this!

LES. *(back to phone)* I'll be right there. *(Hangs up, and starts out to bedroom thru DSR arch.)*

BESS. *(Crosses up, yelling toward bedroom.)* Call Harrison! He'll get him.

LES. *(exiting)* Harrison won't be up. Lawyers don't get up til 9:30.

BESS. Darling, would you please call him. That's what we pay him for.

(Phone rings. BESS answers it above the credenza. LES re-enters and dials phone at desk.)

BESS. Hello. No David, your father had not left yet. A pair of shoes? What happened to your shoes? Uhhh David, your father can't come now. He'll be down after the show. I don't care who you're in a cell with. Maybe you'll learn to drive more carefully.

LES. Hello Har. Les. Sorry to wake you. *(Turns away to talk soto voce.)*

BESS. David, Harrison will come get you. Harrison is our lawyer. What's the difference if he voted for Nixon or not, he can get you out of jail! You're in no position to be particular. *(Looks at watch.)* Goodbye, David! *(Hangs up and races over to table, flicks on the radio monitor switch.)*

LES. That's right, Har. Fifth precinct. Thanks. *(Hangs up.)*

RADIO. Stay tuned in sixty seconds for Breakfast With Les And Bes, with this morning's special feature, an exclusive interview with Princess Grace and Prince Ranier of

Monaco. But first.... *(BESS flicks the switch off.)*

BESS. Is everything OK with Harrison?

LES. *(Crosses DR, then over to coffee table, picks up cup and crosses left to cabinet.)* He'll get him....

BESS. *(pacing, CS)* This is it! I have had it with David's shenanigans. I am tired of having *our* name in the paper every time *he* hits somebody in the mouth who doesn't agree with him or bangs into someone else's car. The station is tired of it. The paper is tired of it and I'm tired of it.

LES. *(Pours more coffee for himself and fills a cup for BESS.)* But the public loves it.

BESS. *(Sits C chair at table.)* That's the point!

LES. What's the point? I thought you wanted publicity! *(Hands her the cup.)*

BESS. Not *bad* publicity.

LES. *(Sits at L of table.)* Ohh the public doesn't care whether it's bad publicity or good publicity. As a matter of fact, they *prefer* bad publicity.

(Yellow warning light on monitor console flashes.)

BESS. But the station doesn't. *(She flicks on the monitor switch.)*

LES. Well, then the station doesn't understand publicity.	ANNOUNCER. It's 8:05 and time for Breakfast With Les And Bess.
BESS. You don't understand. You don't want to understand.	With Bess Christen.........
LES. What do you	and Les Dischinger........

mean, I don't want to un-
derstand.

So, let's go up to their cozy apartment, here in

BESS. It means what it
means. You don't want
to understand.

Manhattan.........

LES. *I* understand,
you're the one who....

and

BESS. *I* don't unders-
tand pub....

have some breakfast.

(Red, "On air" light goes on.)

BESS. *(Flicks off monitor switch.)* Good morning darling.

LES. Good morning dear! *(He picks up the "Variety" again, sips coffee, eats cookies, looks generally disinterested which only serves to annoy BESS. She ignores him, as usual, determined to give her audience a good show.)*

BESS. Well, it's an exciting, exciting morning, isn't it? In a little while we'll be getting a call from Monaco and we'll be talking "live" with Princess Grace and her husband, Prince Ranier.

LES. Isn't it pronounced Ran-yeh?

BESS. *(This catches her off-guard, but only for a second.)* You know ... I'm not really sure. That's one thing we'll have to ask them.

LES. You know something I'd like to ask her?

BESS. *(apprehensively)* What's that?

LES. Well, she had this terrific movie career. And overnight ... it stops. She marries this prince and ... I just wonder if she had ... you know ... trouble adjusting.

BESS. Ohhhh I'm sure she has more than enough to

do. I mean after all she's running a country. Helping to run a country.

LES. That's not what I call a country. It's a bunch of casinos and a beach. It's a resort.

BESS. *(angry, but trying not to show it)* It has a government. It still has to be run.

LES. Well, they probably have bureaucrats for that. This is the Prince and Princess. They probably have to find things to do .. right?

BESS. *(over-compensating)* Ohhh Les *(laugh)* you might as well say that ... that because the Queen of England has the Prime Minister ... and Parliament ... she has to find things to do.

LES. That's probably true.

BESS. *(determined to win the "battle")* Just because an office is ceremonial doesn't mean that there's nothing to do. Ceremony is important. It's very important.

LES. I don't know. I think it would get to you after a while. I think you can open just so many supermarkets.

BESS. I doubt if they have supermarkets in Monaco.

LES. They have supermarkets everywhere.

BESS. I doubt if Princess Grace opens them.

LES. Well, OK!... So she opens a new casino .. or .. an orphanage. I just don't think it can be the same thing as working.

BESS. *(a sweet but definite warning)* Well, do me a favor, Les ... don't ask her that question.

LES. .... OK.

BESS. I'll tell you what I'm going to ask her.

LES. *(with feigned enthusiasm)* What?

BESS. *(holding up her hand as if to say "enough")* Well, she's obviously radiantly happy. But ... I think we'd all like to know ... what it's *really* like to be a princess ... in this day and age ... I mean there are certain realities I'm sure ... it's difficult to leave all your friends behind. And family....

LES. Especially when you come from a very rich family.

BESS. It's still hard. I remember when you left St. Louis. You didn't want to come to New York.

LES. Ahhhh but I was in love. I *had* to be with *you*!

BESS. And Grace ... had to be with him.

LES. Yes! She gave up Hollywood for love. I gave up St. Louis! We're kindred souls!

BESS. *(Laughs again for her listeners.)* She seemed a lot happier giving up Hollywood than you did giving up St. Louis.

LES. Well, I had a good job! Broadcasting the Brownies games. I was *the* announcer. She was just another actress.

BESS. Oh yes... *(another charming laugh)*

LES. If I hadn't come to New York in '41 to see the Yankees-Dodgers series, I might still be out there!

BESS. *(smiling)* If I hadn't met you at a party afterwards, you might still be out there. You were soooo cute. It was all these show-business people. And you looked like some awkward rube. It was formal! It was a show opening. And you were wearing a plaid jacket and white socks.

LES. Caught your eye, huh?

BESS. I don't remember what you were doing there.

LES. The Brownie's owner's brother had money in the show. He sent me to check it out. The show was a bomb. Party was great. I met Melvyn Douglas. And Claudette

Colbert. And Margaret Sullivan...

BESS. And me.

LES. And you. *(There is a pause, as they actually look at each other for a second, caught in remembering.)*

BESS. Speaking of parties, we went to a party last night.

LES. We sure did...

BESS. I haven't seen that many divinely dressed women in one place since the Coty Awards. I think my favorite was the one Dina Merrill had on. It was soooo simple. It was soooo simple. Well, of course she could wear anything.

LES. A plaid jacket with white socks! *(He rises to pour himself more coffee.)*

BESS. You know, I think she could. *(Laughs for her listeners.)* Actually Gloria Vanderbilt did have on a little plaid jacket. It was *gorgeous.* A little silk jacket ... in light yellows and pink plaid ... that fit over this long delicious pink chiffon dress. Just stunning. OH .. and Claire Booth Luce had this breathtakingly simple little purple number. Do you notice how daring women are getting with colors?

LES. *(More fake enthusiasm, he sits again.)* Yes! What are we going to do about it???

BESS. Oh Les .. I saw you chatting with Henry Luce .. *(to audience)* the publisher of Time Magazine. What were you two talking about?

(ROGER EVERSON, in boxer shorts, now enters from DSR bedroom. He's looking for the bathroom. He sees them and tiptoes to the USR bedroom door.)

LES. The Yankees.

BESS. Noooo!

LES. Yes. Whether Mantle and Maris were going to break Babe Ruth's record.

BESS. What did *he* think?

(ROGER now crosses to the front door US, opens it and looks out.)

LES. Well, you know *Time* magazine. He kind of hedged.

(ROGER closes the front door a little too loudly — he's caught. LES and BESS both look. Dead air.)

ROGER. *(UC)* Uh ... pardon me,.. which way is the bathroom?

BESS. *(a little stunned but composed)* I .... think now it's time for a word from New Day Dairys....

(The commercial goes on, indicated by red light going off.)

ROGER. *(suddenly realizing they are on the air)* Ohhhh, I'm sorry. I forgot... You're on radio. Oh Geeze .. I'm sorry. I'll find it. *(He starts off, DR.)*

LES. Hold it! *(He rises and crosses U to C.)* Who are you?

ROGER. Roger Everson. Ensign Everson, U.S. Navy. You can't tell from this. (Indicates underwear.)

BESS. Where do you come from?

ROGER. Well, our home port is Norfolk, but...

LES. Are you a friend of David's??

ROGER. Who's David?

BESS. Shelby?

ROGER. *(smiles)* Uhhhh, yes.

LES. You're a friend of Shelby's.

ROGER. Well, not a friend, exactly.

LES. If you're not a friend, what the hell are you doing here???

ROGER. Well ... I came here to meet you.

BESS. Why should she bring some stranger to meet us? Is your mother a big fan or something???

LES. We don't play Norfolk.

BESS. He's stationed in Norfolk. His mother could live in New Jersey.

ROGER. *(stepping in, next to sofa)* No, my mother lives in Utah.

LES. Why would Shelby bring somebody from Utah to get our autograph for his mother?

BESS. And he's not dressed.

LES. *(Crosses back to table and sits.)* I don't think he "just" came here to meet us. I think she brought him home for something else.

BESS. Why would she bring him *here*? If Shelby was going to do something outrageous like that, she wouldn't do it *here*.

LES. It makes it more outrageous if she does do it here.

BESS. *(Turns, smiles at ROGER, who smiles back.)* Did Shelby bring you home from that party???

ROGER. What party, Mam?

BESS. The party she's been at for the last two days.

ROGER. She wasn't at any party, Mam. She was with me.

LES. Well, then he's no stranger.

BESS. What were you doing together for two days?

LES. Uhh, Bess ... you don't have to *ask* that.

BESS. *(Rises, steps to C.)* Yes I do. What were you doing together for two days?

(Yellow light flashes on panel.)

LES. Bess, the warning light.

ROGER. Well, uh ... uh .... uh ...

LES. Bess, five seconds.   BESS. Yes???

ROGER. We were .. getting married.

(LES sees red "on air" light go on. But both are shocked. Long pause.
BESS just stares... LES recovers.)

LES. *(Rises, leans into microphone.)* Hi. We're back. But ...
we're gonna have to go way again. So ... how about if we
take another quick message here from the people at
Madison Furs!

(Red light goes off. Then immediately the studio phone lights up
and buzzes.)

LES. *(into phone)* Sorry, we need some time here.
(hangs up)

BESS. Did you say, you were getting *married*?

ROGER. Yes, Mam.

BESS. To each other??

ROGER. Yes, Mam.

BESS. *(to LESS)* Get Shelby.

LES. "Yes, Mam." *(He goes to bedroom, DSR thru arch. BESS, alone with ROGER, as he stands, awkwardly.*

BESS. *(fastening her robe more securely)* We have a radio program.

ROGER. Yes, Mam, I know.... I'm sorry to have disturbed it. If you like, ... I'd be glad to go back to bed.

BESS. *(quickly)* No ...... but ... uh ... you might put something else on. There's a robe of Les's in the bathroom.

ROGER. Where *is* the bathroom?

BESS. *(She points.)* It's ... two lefts.

ROGER. Right. *(starts)* Oh ... I've got a robe of my own. *(He goes US to suitcase near the front door, as SHELBY enters from DR, with LES. BESS points US to ROGER.)*

SHELBY. Ohhhh no! *(She goes to ROGER.)* Ohhh Roger, I'm sorry. This is soooo embarrassing.

BESS. Shelby, is this true?

SHELBY. Yes.

BESS. *(Crosses US to just below center steps.)* Why didn't you tell us??

SHELBY. *(at railing with ROGER on her R)* Well, it just happened.

BESS. *Before.* Why didn't you tell us about it, before? Tell us about him, before. Let us meet him before you married him???

SHELBY. Well, I haven't known him that long.

BESS. How long have you known Him?

(Yellow warning light flashes.)

SHELBY. Well.......

LES. *(at R)* Warning light.

BESS. *(Crosses to LES.)* Ohhh God, how are we going to do the program?

LES. Don't! This is much more important.

BESS. This is an *important* program. Princess Grace is going to call any minute! I can't....

(Red "on air" light comes on.)

BESS. *(Staggers to table, quite frazzled.)* Hello again ... well ... well ..... I thought it might be a good idea ... to .. uh ... to uh .... to uh ..... *(Looks to LES.)*

LES. Punt!

BESS. *(finding folder)* To read some of the letters from our adorable refugee children. We know how much you love hearing them ... and we have got quite a few wonderful ones this morning. *(She rustles thru papers looking for letters.)*

LES. *(from across the room)* Why don't we go off? We have backup tapes.

BESS. *(Pushes the squelch button on the microphone.)* Not today! *(Finds letter and sits in L chair.)* Ahhh here they are! Here's one we just got yesterday from our own little foster child in Korea... *(LES gets wooden file box from credenza and crosses to table, sits.)*

SHELBY. *(loud whisper)* We're going back to bed! *(She and ROGER start for the DSR arch.)*

BESS. Hi Shelb! Our daughter, Shelby, is up! Wait a minute, Shelby honey, ... I want to talk to you. Find out what *you've* been up to. And, we'll do that right after we hear some of these wonderful letters. *(SHELBY and RO-GER stand impatiently. LES is looking through file.)* **All right! Let's see ... the letter from our foster child in Korea, Mo Ching. We just call him "Mo."**

LES. **That's his real name.**

BESS. *(She gives him a "look.")* **Now ... "Dear Foster Parents... Today was bright and sunny. the sun was bright on the lake."** *(SHELBY and ROGER start off again and exit DSR, SHELBY leading him out.)*

BESS. **Uh .... we'll finish this letter ... and of course any minute we'll be hearing from Princess Grace. But let's now hear from ...** *(checks list)* **"Firmwear Fashions."**

(Red light off.)

BESS. *(Goes toward bedroom, gets SHELBY on way.)* **Shelby, you come back in here this instant. We can talk during the program. We can talk during the commercials. You've *got* to explain all this.** *(She leads SHELBY to the sofa, they sit, and ROGER sits in the DSR armchair.)*

SHELBY. **I'll explain it! I'll explain it, but I'm not going to sit here and explain it a minute at a time! We'll talk after the show!** *(She starts to get up — BESS sits her down.)*

LES. *(finding a file card)* **No. Let's talk right now. We'll get them to play the interview we did with Bernstein we never ran.**

BESS. **No! We're interviewing Princess Grace later, we can't have two interviews on the same show!!!**

LES. **We can't???** *(He picks up the studio phone. Into phone.)* **Ken?? Look. We've got some problems on this end. Would you run the May 16 Bernstein tape? When Prin-**

cess Grace calls, we'll cut back in. Right. Do it!

BESS. *(rises)* Les this program is too important. Steiner is *listening* this morning.

LES. *(rises)* I think our daughter is more important.

BESS. Of course our daughter is more important. But she can wait. The show can't!

LES. *(Crosses R in front of BESS, sits on sofa next to SHELBY.)* Well, *I* can't wait. I'm dying of curiosity!

(Yellow warning light flashes.)

BESS. *(CS)* Shelby, you understand the problem here. A lot of talk shows have been cancelled. And we have an interview coming up with Princess Grace, so I can't just stop and talk to you, but I *do* want to know what this is all about....

(Red light on.)

LES. *(whispers)* We're on. *(Crosses to mike.)* HI! .... Have *we* got a treat for you. Bess just realized that we never got to play the wonderful interview we did with Leonard Bernstein, backstage at the Philharmonic. So today you're going to get two interviews for the price of one. First Lenny ... and then the Royal Couple. Here *he* is first.

(Red light off.)

BESS. *(She is CS, steaming.)* That *wasn't* smart. Steiner's not going to like it!

LES. Steiner's daughter didn't just spring a marriage

on him! NOW ... Daughter O Mine. Spill Da Beans!

SHELBY. What do you want to know?

LES. Well, ... how about *everything*?

SHELBY. There's nothing more to tell. We're married!

LES. Yes, well there are a *few* details you left out. Like who is he?

SHELBY. Don't talk about Roger like he's not here. Ask *him* who he is. *(LES starts to cross in for an argument.)*

BESS. *(Stops him and interrupts.)* Can we please start from the beginning? *(pause)* Who are you, Roger?

ROGER. *(rises)* I'm an Ensign in the U.S. Navy.

BESS. We *know* that. Where did you two meet?

SHELBY. *(Looks lovingly at ROGER.)* In Bermuda. When I was there on vacation.

BESS. You didn't mention meeting him.

SHELBY. I know. It was.... Do I have to tell you about everyone I meet?

BESS. *(shouting)* Only when you're thinking of marrying them.

SHELBY. *(shouting back)* I wasn't thinking of marrying him then.

LES. *(controlling BESS)* OK! So you met in Bermuda, and you've been seeing each other since then.

SHELBY. Yes.

ROGER. *(overlapping)* No. *(They look at each other.)*

LES. *You've* been seeing *him* but *he* hasn't been seeing *you.*

SHELBY. Well, not exactly .. y'see ....

LES. You were seeing each other but it wasn't serious.

SHELBY. Well .... no .... uh ....

BESS. Les, let *her* explain.

LES. *(Takes a step back.)* OK!! Fine.

SHELBY. Well ... um .... um ... uh .... *(Looks to ROGER.)* Well ... you see ...... we ...... uh ... *(giggles)*

LES. I was doing a better job than she is.

BESS. LES!

LES. Well she's *not* explaining anything. Roger, give me a straight, succinct naval explanation.

ROGER. Uhhhhh, well, we met in Bermuda.

LES. Uh huh.

ROGER. Our last day there.

LES. Uh huh.

ROGER. And I went to sea.

LES. Right.

ROGER. And I came back yesterday.

LES. That's .. one day in Bermuda. That's yesterday. That's today. That's three days. You've known each other for three days. *(Crosses L to cabinet.)*

BESS. THREE DAYS???? THREE DAYS???? You knew each other three days before you got married???

ROGER. Well, actually only two *before*.....

LES. Two, three, what's a day among friends? *(Pours himself coffee, sits at table.)*

BESS. *(CS, absolutely beside herself)* TWO DAYS??? TWO DAYS??? Shelby, how can you marry someone you've only known for two days?

SHELBY. Well ... um .... I love him.

BESS. *(leaning in on sofa arm)* How can you *love* somebody you've only known for two days???

SHELBY. I loved him after five minutes!

LES. You didn't love him at first sight??

SHELBY. No, it's not how he looks. *(Rises, crosses to*

ROGER, takes his hand.) It's what he *did*!

BESS. *(Crosses to them, R, between sofa and coffee table.)*
What, pray tell, did he *do*???

ROGER. Oh, it was nothing, Mam.

BESS. Ohhhhh, I wanna *know*! *(Sits on sofa.)*

SHELBY. *(Crosses in, to corner of sofa.)* I rented one of those
motor bikes down in Bermuda, y'know and my skirt got
caught in the chain and I was trying to pull it out and
screaming and being all hysterical and he just came over
and he said, "What are you wearing under your skirt?"
And I said ... a little shocked at first ... I said, "My bathing
suit." And he said, "Well, why don't you step out of the
skirt?" And I *did*.. I just thought that was soooo terrific.
(She waits for reaction.)

BESS. *(Looks to LES. His head sinks onto the table.)* And that
was it?? You were in love?

SHELBY. I know it doesn't sound like much, but you
had to be there. I was *really hysterical.* And he was just so
practical. I loved him.

BESS. *(Stumbles as she rises.)* And how practical do you
think it is to marry him after just two days? *(Crosses to
table.)*

SHELBY. Oh *that's* not practical, at all. That was *my* idea.
As soon as he got off the ship, and I saw him, I got hysterical ... and said, "Let's get married."

BESS. Roger, why didn't you say something *practical
then.*

ROGER. *(Crosses C, above sofa, to BESS.)* I did, Mam. I
said, "I'd like to get to know you better." And she said,
"Know schmo. This is the real thing. Let's go with it."

BESS. And *that* convinced you???

ROGER. Well, that and .... you know ... I'd been at sea for two months.

BESS. Oh ... terrific. *(Sinks into C chair at table.)*

ROGER. But *that's* practical!

SHELBY. *(Crosses in, stands at Roger's R.)* Mom, Dad, what's the big deal? Three days can be three years to some people.

LES. That's lovely poetry, honey, but it doesn't usually make a happy marriage.

SHELBY. You and Mom knew each other for a year.

LES. Yeah, well....

SHELBY. Princess Grace and Prince Ranier hardly knew each other at all.

BESS. *(Rises, crosses DR, to fireplace.)* Yes, but, Shelby, they both came from good families!

SHELBY. Our family's not that bad.

BESS. *Roger's* family. We don't *know* him.

SHELBY. Roger's family is fine!

BESS. How do you know? You never met them.

SHELBY. What difference does it make if *he's* wonderful!

BESS. *(Crosses in, below sofa, kneels on it, leaning in toward SHELBY.)* Shelby honey, maybe ... you could get it annulled .. and we...

SHELBY. *(outraged)* I'm not getting it annulled. I'm not getting anything annulled. I am married, and I am married for good. *(BESS sits on sofa.)* You don't seem to understand that. And ... you're embarrassing me in front of my husband. I brought him here to be introduced, not .. cross-examined!

LES. *(Rises, crosses in, to ROGER'S L.)* Shelby honey, we're sorry, but .. you don't bring strangers home as husbands and then not expect us to be upset. You just don't do that.

SHELBY. Well *I* do it. You should know me by now!! Look, Mother. Father. This is Roger. He is my husband. Now that is that. Will you please consider him your son ... and try to love him .. starting as soon as possible. Please. *(SHELBY grabs ROGER and they cross above the sofa and exit quickly to bedrooms. LES and BESS are still in shock for a moment.)*

(The bedroom door slams.)

BESS. *(Rises, crosses to table.)* We'll have it annulled. She's under age.

LES. Wait a minute. He might be a terrific guy.

BESS. Les, for God's sake. *(sits)*

LES. *(Crosses R.)* What did she do? She got married on impulse. I think people oughta do *more* things on impulse.

BESS. I'm going to get it annulled.

LES. *(Crosses back to her, at C.)* Why don't you *think* about it first?

SHELBY. *(Enters from DR arch to below dofa.)* And if you're thinking about getting it annulled, *forget it*! I'll fight it. I'll fight it in the courts. I'll get the best lawyers money can buy. You've run my life up to now. Now it's *my* turn. Roger's gonna run my life!

ROGER. *(Enters, crosses to SHELBY.)* Shelb ... why don't you calm down ... and come back to bed.

SHELBY. I know them, they're gonna try to get it annulled.

ROGER. We can talk about this later.

SHELBY. They'll have done it by then!!! *(She pushes past him and sits in DR armchair. ROGER follows her.)*

(Front door opens and DAVID enters in wet and dirty tuxedo and bare feet.)

DAVID. *(mouths)* Gooood morning. *(SHELBY has started to cry and is comforted by ROGER.)*

BESS. *(Goes to SHELBY, kneels on floor beside her.)* Shelby honey, ... you're tired ... you're overwrought...

DAVID. *(Closes door, at C railing, checks his watch.)* Heyyyy ... it's eight-forty, how come you're not on the air?

LES. *(L of C)* We *are* on the air! We've got a crisis here ... now wait your turn!

DAVID. *(Steps DRC.)* What's the matter? Hey Shelby .. what'd *you* do?

BESS. *(Holds her hand up to stop him.)* She just got married.

DAVID. *(Crosses C, above sofa, laughing.)* This morning? On the air? What you people won't do for an audience.

ROGER. *(Steps in, to David.)* We got married yesterday!

DAVID. Who are you?

LES. The husband.

ROGER. *(Shakes hands with David.)* I'm Roger Everson, U.S. Navy.

DAVID. *(to LES)* She married a sailor?? *(Crosses DR to SHELBY.)* Shelby, you married a sailor?

SHELBY. YES I MARRIED A SAILOR!!!! AND I'M STAYING MARRIED.

ROGER. *(stepping in)* I'm not a sailor. I'm a naval officer.

(DAVID laughs and moves DS, then crosses to above sofa.)

BESS. David, go get out of those wet clothes. You're dripping on the carpet!

LES. Is that *my* tuxedo???

DAVID. Yes.

LES. You've ruined it!

DAVID. You ought to see the car.

LES. *(Chases DAVID, who runs up C above railing.)* It's *your* car. That's *my* tuxedo!!!

BESS. David ... get out of those clothes. We'll deal with you later.

DAVID. *(at L of center, in front of desk)* What time do the evening papers come?

BESS. Why?

DAVID. *(sheepishly)* I think my picture's in the *Post.*

BESS. Oh God! No! No! No! No! No! *(as she crawls along the floor, pounding her fist and collapses between the sofa and the coffee table)*

DAVID. I think so. That's America for you. When I picket a United State's senator's office for the way he votes on civil rights, no one takes my picture. But drive into *one* lake... *(Leans on railing.)*

BESS. *(face buried in the carpet)* You're impossible.

DAVID. I'm not impossible. The press is impossible. We've got to reform the press in this country.

BESS. *(Rises, crosses U to L of DAVID.)* How about reforming yourself first? *(Wheels on LES.)* Lester, this is *your* fault. You don't discipline your son.

DAVID. It's not Dad's fault. I'm an adult. I'm responsible for my own behavior.

LES. *(at DSR end of railing)* Nooo, it's my fault. I should have made sure you didn't have those car keys.

DAVID. Nooo, it's not your fault. That would be a childish way to treat me. I respect your not taking the keys and treating me like an adult.

BESS. What good does it do to treat you like an adult when you act like a child?

DAVID. What good does it do to treat me like a child when I act like a child!? If you treat me like an adult, you got a fighting chance.

SHELBY. *(Rises, runs UC to railing.)* Will everyone *please*, please, please, please stop this. I just got married. *(They look at Roger.)* I wanna celebrate. I don't want fights.

BESS. *(Crosses U to SHELBY.)* Ohhh honey, we're not fighting about *you.* We're happy for you.

LES. I thought you were upset about her.

BESS. Yes, of course I'm upset about her. But I'm happy for her.

SHELBY. *(Crosses DR, dives into sofa, burys head in pillows.)* I don't understannnnnnnnnnnnnnnnnnnnd!

BESS. *(Crosses D, kneels at L side of sofa.)* Oh, honey... what I mean is .. I'm upset because I'm a romantic. I wanted you to have a big church wedding. That's all. I'm sure Roger's a fine... I'm sure, Roger, you're a fine young man, but Mr. Dischinger and I ... we got married on the spur of the moment in New Haven. We had dinner with an old college professor of his ... from Missouri .. who was then at Yale .. and all through dinner he kept saying, ... "You make such a lovely couple .. you make such a lovely couple." So, before we went back to New York, we got married.

LES. *(Crosses D, sits on end table, leaning in, toward*

SHELBY.) We opened in New Haven.

BESS. That's right, isn't it? We did .... but we were married in his living room. In the professor's living room, by a Common Pleas Court Judge....

LES. Named Merriman..... *(another moment of remembering between them)*

BESS. Named Merriman.. and I had on a suit. A green suit. So .... I'm ... a romantic .. I wanted something more for you, just like all the other silly mothers. *(Crosses L, to table, sits C chair.)*

SHELBY. *(Sits up.)* That's not .. silly....

DAVID. That's not, Mother....

LES. Oh yes it is. Your mother *is* a romantic. Or was.

DAVID. Noooo, that's not romance. That's PR. That's page one of the society column of the *Times.*

BESS. David, that's cruel. When you get married, I'd like you to have a big wedding, too.

DAVID. You probably want it on the program to hype the ratings.

LES. "Hype the ratings???"

DAVID. Yeah. I read the "trades." On the toilet. Talk shows are doomed. ABC's all music. NBC's all music. Rock and roll. It's coming.

BESS. Talk shows are not doomed! Nothing is doomed unless you neglect it!

DAVID. Like us....!

BESS. *(Crosses U to center steps.)* YOU ... change your clothes .. and get off to school. Shelby and Roger, go back to bed. Roger, you can use the guest room! *(Crosses D to table.)*

SHELBY. Mother, we're married!

BESS. *(Looks at LES. Pause.)* Yes .... of course ... *(They all start out.)*

SHELBY. Good night! *(SHELBY and ROGER exit DSR arch.)*

DAVID. Good morning. *(He exits thru USR arch. LES and BESS are alone again. Bess sinks into chair at table and starts to cry.)*

(Studio phone buzzes and lights up.)

LES. *(Crosses L, to table, picks up studio phone.)* Yes? Oh?? Oh ... Uh .. OK ... give us a signal. *(Hangs up.)* Tapes almost out. We have to wrap it up. *(Pours more coffee at cabinet.)*

BESS. They didn't call!

LES. Huh?

BESS. Princess Grace... They didn't call!!

LES. Damn lucky thing.

BESS. We told everyone they'd call!

LES. Well, tell em they'll call some other time.

BESS. That's a terrible thing to do to your audience. Promise them something. Get them all listening. And then not deliver.

LES. It's not our fault. It's Princess Grace's fault. SHE didn't call.

BESS. The listeners don't care whose fault it is. We let them down.

LES. She let us down.

BESS. They don't know that!

LES. We'll tell them. We're going on any second. We'll tell em.

BESS. No, no, no. We can't do that. We'll ... make up a
story. We'll say ... something came up. Something very
glamorous. She had to .. uh... She had to attend the opening of the Royal Regatta .. they'll .. understand that.

LES. *(Sits at table.)* Why not just tell them the phones got
screwed up, they'll understand that better!

BESS. You don't think she forgot? Ohhh God. And
after all the nice things I wrote about her when she was an
actress. How could she just forget?

LES. I'm sure she didn't forget!

BESS. You don't think it was intentional! I ... did .. *once,*
in one review, say a performance of her's was
"wooden."

LES. They are three thousand miles away. Who knows
what happened. Maybe their baby's sick. Maybe they're
taking care of their baby.

BESS. They have nurses for that.

LES. Not always. Some people actually take care of
their own children!!

(Yellow warning light flashes.)

LES. We're on ... in five...

(Pause, then red "on air" light comes on.)

BESS. Well ... wasn't that an absolutely divine interview
with Leonard Bernstein?

LES. He's as articulate as he is ... uh .. musical.

BESS. The most articulate musican I know.

LES. Yes.

BESS. Yes. *(She can't go on, still affected by everything that's happened. They seem frozen; suddenly LES jumps in.)*

LES. You know, it reminds me of a story about Yasha Heifitz.

BESS. Oh?

LES. Yes.... He was once recording a .. I don't know .. a Beethoven concerto .. and ... uh ... he made ... like three takes ... and at the end of the day .. the engineer came into the studio .. and said, "Mr. Heifitz ... on that second movement .. I think you made a mistake on bar 3." Heifitz looked at him .. nodded ... and asked, "Did I make that mistake on *all three takes?*" The engineer said, "Yes." Heifitz said, "Well, I guess that's the way I play it!!!!"

BESS. *(She laughs for real.)* I never heard that one.

LES. I don't tell you everything.

BESS. *(Takes off her watch, looks at it.)* Well, I see it's almost time to go. Oh, and I do want to apologize to all our listeners. We had promised you the live interview with Princess Grace and Prince Ranier.

LES. Ran-yeh. *(He rises and stands at cabinet.)*

BESS. But ... there must have been some problem with the trans-atlantic cable.... We *are* certain that we *will* have them on the air ... I'm sure in the next few days ... so ... I'll be speaking to Princess Grace myself and let you all know.... I'm sure those of you who've had phone troubles will understand .. and I'm sure you'll all tune in tomorrow to find out *(stretching for time)* when she'll be talking to us in her exclusive live-on-air interview, direct from her ... very Royal palace ... in very glamorous Monaco. So, until tomorrow ... have a good day...!

(Red light goes off. BESS flicks on the monitor switch.)

RADIO. Beep! It's nine o'clock and time for the latest news. *(BESS turns it off. There is a pause while both just catch their breath, for just having made it through.)*

(Phone rings.)

BESS. *(Crosses R, above sofa, answers phone. Into phone.)* Yes? Hi Bob. I don't know what happened. I was just going to call Monaco and see. I'm sure it was just... *(She continues sotto voce as, from UR arch, DAVID enters, crossing to door in jeans, dirty sneakers, etc.)*

LES. *(Crosses to C.)* Hold it!

DAVID. I'm late for class.

LES. This won't take long.

DAVID. I could cut class.

LES. It *won't* take long.

BESS. *(Holds phone, turns to LES.)* Are you going to *talk* to him?

LES. I was about to. Would you like to join?

BESS. I'm sweet-talking Steiner. *(Punches button.)* I'll take it in the bedroom. *(She crosses to UR arch as DAVID crosses DR to armchair.)*

BESS. Be firm!

LES. You too! *(She exits. He turns to DAVID.)*

DAVID. *(plopping into chair)* Dad, I'm sorry. I couldn't help it. This girl I was with just thought I was a spoiled rich kid. I really wanted to show her that I really don't care about money.

LES. *(Crosses DS.)* So you drowned the car.

DAVID. It worked. She was very impressed.

LES. I'm glad. *(Crosses to DAVID.)* Look. I don't mind that you're a rebellious kid. A little rebellious is healthy. A lot is *sick.* You do have to grow up!

DAVID. Not yet. I'm still young.

LES. David, I'm serious. We can't have this kind of thing anymore. Maybe you should see a psychiatrist.

DAVID. I *am* seeing a psychiatrist.

LES. Well, what does he say?

DAVID. He doesn't say *anything.* I do all the talking.

LES. What does he *think?* What do you talk about? Is it any help?

DAVID. He *thinks* I should move out of here. We *talk* about me and you and mom, and it's *no help* whatsoever! *(Checks watch.)* I'm late. Gotta go. *(Crosses UC to door.)*

LES. *(following him)* David, you can't cut off a conversation like this.

DAVID. Why not? My shrink does it all the time. *(And he goes out front door.)*

BESS. *(Enters from bedrooms, crosses D to sofa.)* Well, Steiner was upset. He said we should have called *them* as soon as they hadn't called us. I told him I didn't think it was polite to "bug" the Royal family. He said Royal family-schmamly! *(She collapses on couch.)*

LES. *(Moves down to R edge of couch.)* Bess, how long has David been seeing a psychiatrist?

BESS. *(pause)* Ten years.

LES. Ten years??? What's wrong with him??

BESS. *(Sits up.)* How can you *say* that. Look how he behaves.

LES. I *know* how he behaves. I wanna know what's

wrong. After ten years shouldn't we know what's wrong? Shouldn't we get a report or something?

BESS. What's wrong is very simple. Lack of discipline.

LES. Ah!

BESS. *(stage whisper)* Why do you think Shelby married a military man. She wants *discipline!*

LES. *(pacing at fireplace)* I thought maybe she wanted attention. Love. It seems to me you don't drive into a lake in Central Park or get married on the spur of the moment unless you want someone to notice you. I mean that's kind of psychology 101, but... *(BESS is distracted.)* Is something wrong? Bess?

BESS. *(She turns.)* We've certainly messed up our kids, haven't we? '

LES. Well, it's not *entirely* our fault.

BESS. Thank God.

LES. But I do think .. and I know you're not going to want to hear this.... I think the trouble really began when the program began.

BESS. Oh, please!

LES. How long have we been on the air? Ten years. How long has David been in therapy? Ten years!

BESS. Oh, Lester! That's ... that's just a coincidence! A child's most impressionable years are when their four five and six. We weren't on the air *then*!! Why must you blame *everything* on the show?

LES. *(Crosses U, above sofa to table at L.)* Because I think that before it, we were happy. Oh yeah, we were away a lot. I was working on my column and you worked on yours, but we were happy ... and the kids felt it. But this... *(Refers to radio setup, then crosses back to R of sofa.)* ...this public life .. saps us. Don't you see that??

BESS. *I'm* happy. I love it.

LES. *(Shakes his head, sighs, frustrated, turns.)* Bess, I've got a great idea. Why don't *we* do something impulsive. Let's tell Steiner we quit.

BESS. You think the "trades" are right. Do you think our show is doomed?

LES. What do they know? They said TV would kill radio. Radio's still here.

BESS. Music is not radio!

LES. *(Sits on R arm of sofa.)* I don't know about these things. Somewhere a guy invents a jet plane. The next thing you know, the Dodgers leave town. Nobody saw the connection till it happened. Everything's changing. Maybe *we* ought to.

BESS. I don't want to change. I like things the way they are. You like things the way they *were.*

LES. I liked being in love with you. I liked doing something satisfying with my life. I can't want that again??? *(He comes to her.)* Bess, look. We could start now. Take a year off. Do something crazy. Shake up our lives.

BESS. I couldn't take a year off.

LES. *(Sits next to her on sofa.)* We'll start small. We'll take a week off. We'll go out to San Francisco. You love San Francisco. We can watch Willy Mays. He's not gonna be there forever.

BESS. Les, that's no solution.

LES. OK. Smaller! We'll start smaller. Tonight, you and I will go to the fight in Philly. Just like old times. We'll get a room at the Bellvue and...

BESS. We have the refugee children.

LES. They've been refugees this long, they can wait one more night!

BESS. I can't.

LES. *(He turns her around ... and quietly.)* How about it? We'll start small ... tonight .. in Philadelphia.

BESS. *(There is a long pause as she briefly considers it, but then she recovers and it's back to business as usual.)* I ..... I've got to call Monaco. *(And she moves away, UR, and to the bedrooms and out. LES, alone, picks up a newspaper, folds it neatly, but then slams it down on the coffee table and crosses L.)*

(From DSR, ROGER now enters and moves across toward suit-
       case.)

ROGER. Sorry... I forgot my bag. I'll want to get dressed later.

LES. Good idea. *(ROGER starts back with bag. DR LES sees hat on floor where he threw it ... bends ... hands it to him.)* This yours?

ROGER. Oh, yes. Thanks. *(Starts to go, stops.)* Sir, listen, I hope you don't mind what happened with me and Shelby. It was just one of those things. We just felt it was right. Sometimes there are things you just feel you have to do, so you do it! You ... understand?

LES. .... You bet! *(They nod to each other. ROGER turns, exits with suitcase.)*

(Phone rings.)

LES. *(Picks it up. Into phone.)* Hello. Ohhh, hello... Prince ... Your Highness ... whatever. Ohhhh. Oh no, it's all

right. We figured there was something like that. My wife is
trying to get you on the other phone. You will? When? Oh
... OK .. fine .. No.. We understand.. Sure... *(Crosses D, in
front of sofa with the phone.)* There is something I would like
to ask you .. right now. Is it Rainier or Ran-yeh? Ahhhh!
Good. Oh ... and .. if you have a moment... Good, *(He sits.)*
just one more question... Uh... I was just curious .. do you
really like what you do? *(And LES listens .. alone .. on the phone
.. listening to the Prince.)*

(Lights fade to black.)
(The Curtain Falls.)

Intermission

ACT TWO

Scene 1

Time: Early the following morning.

Set: The same, but it is after a party. The dining table has empty
    paper cups (about 2 dozen) and beer bottles on it as well as
    an almost empty bowl of potato chips and a girl's hat. Also a
    couple of ashtrays full of butts. The fireplace mantle is also
    full of empty cups and a half dozen liquor bottles, a cardboard
    box below it into which some debris has already been thrown.
    The coffee table, end table, credenza and desk are also covered
    with assorted cups, bottles and bowls of popcorn. Strewn
    across the center railing are confetti-type streamers. Crepe
    paper streamers and balloons are strung up from wall to wall
    upstage and a banner hangs in the window that reads,
    "Happy Wedding." There also are several large shopping
    bags and cardboard boxes in various locations, into which the
    kids will dump the mess as they clean up during the scene.
    There is also a pile of bottles, cups and food bags on the coun-
    ter in the kitchen and another dozen liquor bottles (mostly
    scotch and whiskey), some with a little liquid left in them, on
    the radio cabinet.

SHELBY, DSR, turns on the vacuum cleaner which has a practical
light on the front and the lights come up. DAVID is dottering
from table to table emptying ashtrays into a woman's hat.
ROGER is asleep on the couch. He sleeps with his hat over his
face. Rock music of the era blares on the stereo. SHELBY is
moving in time with the music. She vacuums past couch, lifts
ROGER'S arm to clean. She sees his watch.

SHELBY. *(shouts)* Heyyyyy! It's seven thirty!

DAVID. *(at credenza)* What??

SHELBY. It's *(Turns off vacuum. Now all we hear is music.)* It's
seven thirty.

DAVID. Great party!

SHELBY. Where are Mom and Dad? *(Crosses to bookcase at
R, turns off stereo.)*

DAVID. They went to their own party!

SHELBY. I *know* that. But where are they??? It's seven-
thirty. They go on the air at eight. I'm worried!

DAVID. *(Crosses L, to table.)* They haven't missed a
show yet.

SHELBY. *(Crosses to railing, removes streamers.)* They're
gonna go through the roof when they see this mess.

DAVID. *(clearing beer bottles off table)* Why? We told 'em we
were gonna have a little wedding party.

SHELBY. Three hundred people is not little!

DAVID. To tell you the truth, I don't know who half the
people were. You ask a few friends .. to bring a few friends
... and suddenly you've got three hundred strangers! *(Puts
the hat on his head.)*

SHELBY. *(Crosses D to C.)* David... Do you think my
friends liked Roger?

DAVID. *(sipping from a left-over beer bottle)* Roger who? *(SHELBY hits him on the arm.)* I don't know.

SHELBY. Come on ... what do you think....

DAVID. I don't think they could help but like him.

SHELBY. Oh?

DAVID. He was asleep most of the time. *(Crosses R, to coffee table, picks up liquor bottles then crosses to end table, picks up silver tray.)*

SHELBY. Well ... he's not used to these hours. *(Turning to prostrate ROGER.)* Are ya, baby? *(to DAVID)* ...you like him, don't you? *(DAVID looks at her, then back to work.)* David .... David? *DAVID?*

DAVID. *(above sofa, gathering bottles on credenza, putting them on tray)* I don't know! I didn't feel strongly one way or the other.

SHELBY. Well .... he ... well ... ah ... you ... you've got to get to know him.

DAVID. You've only known him three days longer than I have! *(Crosses L, to cabinet, arranges all the bottles on top.)*

SHELBY. *(Turns to face DAVID.)* David, you don't understand. He's good for me, David. He's steel. He's wood. He's iron. And I'm feathers. You know that, I'm feathers. You're feathers. Our whole family is feathers.

DAVID. Shelby, you marry to love someone, if possible ... *not* because their dullness balances your insanity.

SHELBY. *(Looks at ROGER.)* He isn't dull — he's — *stable.*

DAVID. Whatever!

SHELBY. And he's going to stabilize me!

DAVID. What's wrong with staying the way you are?

SHELBY. *(Steps toward DAVID.)* I'm *not* happy this way.

DAVID. Sure you are.

SHELBY. No I'm not.

DAVID. Yes you are!!!

SHELBY. Are you trying to tell me whether I'm happy or not?

DAVID. I don't have to tell you. If you weren't .. you'd be different.

SHELBY. That's ridiculous. Take an alcoholic. An alcoholic isn't happy. He'd like to change, but he can't help it.

DAVID. An alcoholic is happy. That's the point. Drinking *makes* him happy.

SHELBY. David, you're a psychology major, how can you talk like that???

DAVID. Refreshing, isn't it?

SHELBY. *(She waves him off, crosses to ROGER, looks down at him, as DAVID takes the tray and chip baskets off to the kitchen. ROGER is sleeping. She perches on L arm of sofa.)* You're good for me. You're good for me. You are.

ROGER. *(Opens eyes.)* Uhhh .. uh! Hi.

SHELBY. Good morning.

ROGER. Hmmmm? Oh? *(Sits up.)* Oh noooo. *(He stands up.)* Did I sleep thru the whole party?

SHELBY. *(Stands and comes to him.)* Just the last eight hours.

ROGER. Ahh, I'm sorry, honey. My hours are all turned around, y'know.

SHELBY. It's OK — I love you all turned around. *(They start to embrace and kiss as DAVID enters, interrupting.)*

DAVID. *(Salutes.)* Morning, Captain!

ROGER. Good morning.

(Phone rings. ROGER gets up, straightening his uniform. He moves past bookshelf at R, stops, looks. DAVID answers phone above sofa. SHELBY crosses U, to desk, cleans it off.)

DAVID. *(on phone)* Hello. Who? Prince Rainier. Sure, I'll talk...

SHELBY. Wait a minute, David! *(She makes a tentative move to him to stop him, but waits...)*

DAVID. Heyyyy Prince. How're you doing? This is Napoleon Bonaparte. What say we invade Russia next week? *(He hangs up, laughing and crosses L to table.)* That was Jerry Charney. He's bombed out of his mind.

SHELBY. *(at railing)* David ... I think you ... uh. Oh, never mind.

ROGER. *(Turns from bookshelf with book in hand, which he carries with him thru-out the scene.)* Shelby, how come there are so many copies of *Anna Karenina* on the bookshelf?

SHELBY. Oh, it's my father's favorite book!

ROGER. *(Moves to just below railing.)* Yeah, but twenty-three copies? Most of em are paperbacks.

DAVID. *(At table, cleans up all the cups.)* Well, the truth is he'd never *finished* it. He gets a couple of chapters in .. then puts it down. Then ... he'll be going off on a trip somewhere .. and, he'll have forgotten to take something to read ... so he'll buy another copy of *Anna Karenina* .. and he'll start it again ... on the plane ... and not finish it .. and bring it home .. and he's been going on like that for twenty years.

ROGER. Why doesn't he just give up on it?

SHELBY. He *likes* it!

DAVID. They're home!

(BESS is heard, whistling in the hall; the kids scramble: SHELBY gets the vacuum cleaner and takes it off R, ROGER clears bottles from bookcase and mantle, DAVID tries to finish clearing the table. The front door opens. It's BESS.)

BESS. Hello! What ... what's going on here?

DAVID. Good morning. You're on the air in thirty minutes.

BESS. *(Crosses C.)* I know. I know. What are you doing up? What .. what's been going on here?

SHELBY. *(at DS arch with ROGER US of her.)* I had a party. A wedding party.

BESS. *(looking around)* The place is a mess.

DAVID. *(Crosses DR to fireplace.)* No, *this* is *neat*!

SHELBY. Where's Dad...?

BESS. He's not *here*?

DAVID. No....

BESS. Oh, noooo. *(She throws up her hands in minor despair. Kids stop cleaning and look at her.)*

SHELBY. Mom, what's the matter?

BESS. *(removing her gloves at L corner of credenza)* Nothing is the matter, except that I haven't got the slightest idea where your father is .. that's all.

SHELBY. *(stepping in, to R corner of credenza)* Wasn't he at the party with you?

BESS. Yes, of course.

DAVID. *(Takes last two bottles off mantle.)* What was the party for tonight?

BESS. The Refugee Parents of America...

DAVID. No wonder he disappeared.

BESS. *(overlapping)* But he was in a wonderful mood.

DAVID. There must have been benzadrine in the punch. *(He crosses L, to cabinet with bottles. ROGER gets all cups from bookcase and mantle, then exits to kitchen. SHELBY paces at R, obviously angry with BESS.)*

BESS. *(Crosses to fireplace.)* I don't understand it myself. He was cursing about the party all the way over in the cab. Then he runs into Nate Moody, his old broadcasting friend. They start reminiscing, next thing I know Les is charm itself — he's laughing, joking, chatting with all the old dowagers he usually ignores. He was so good-natured, *(Crosses L, to sofa.)* it frightens me. He even did a song with me, there was a kind of a little show for all the parents. Then all of a sudden he announces that he and Nate are going to Houston, Texas.

SHELBY. *(at R of end table)* Texas? Why would he go to Texas?

(ROGER re-enters, crosses R, to end table, cleans up.)

BESS. Why couldn't he go to 21. Or Toots Shoors?

DAVID. *(cleaning at tea cart)* Maybe he went to see a fight ... or a ballgame or something. *(Exits to kitchen.)*

BESS. Is there a ball team in Texas?

ROGER. *(cleaning at credenza)* No, Mam.

BESS. Thank you, Roger. *(She sits.)*

ROGER. Not professional. The University of Texas has a pretty good team though. *(He collects shopping bags, exits to kitchen.)*

BESS. Thank you, Roger. I have called all of his old hang-outs.

SHELBY. The party didn't go all night, did it?

BESS. Of course not.

SHELBY. *(accusingly)* Where have you been?

BESS. We all went over to Bill Sherwood's for a screening of his new movie.

SHELBY. While Dad was still missing?

BESS. I did everything I could to find him.

DAVID. *(Enters from kitchen with empty box. ROGER also enters, crosses DR, starts to gather all the ballons.)* How was the movie?

BESS. Funny ... but trivial. *(She gets up, whirls anxiously, and crosses above sofa to phone on credenza.)* Maybe I should call the police.

DAVID. *(Crosses D, to R end of coffee table.)* Mom, leave him alone. He'll get it out of his system. Be back to his old self again. *(kneels)*

BESS. David, please. He may have been hit by a cab or mugged or something. I'd better call the police. *(She goes to phone, starts to lift it.)*

DAVID. 444-1-2-3-4. *(And he dumps half of the remaining mess from the coffee table into the box.)*

BESS. *(Looks at him, puts phone down.)* No!

SHELBY. What's the matter?

BESS. If I call, and he hasn't been found ... or picked up for something .. the words going to get around that I called the police, looking for Les ... and you know it's going to get into the papers somehow.

SHELBY. Mother, for once stop worrying about your image, and think about Dad! *(BESS picks up phone.)*

DAVID. *(as he crosses to kitchen with box and exits)* 444-1-2-3-4....

BESS. *(Puts it down again.)* No, if they had picked him up ... they would have called *here.*

SHELBY. Oh mother....

(Phone rings. Everyone freezes, DAVID at kitchen arch, ROGER at desk with armful of ballons. They all stare at the phone. BESS looks to DAVID. He answers it.)

DAVID. Hello. No, this is his son, David.

BESS. *(grabbing DAVID)* Is that the police? Is he all right??? Oh, God, it's the police!

DAVID. It's Mrs. Dalcimer. She wants to know where the Christmas tree lights are. *(The tension is broken. ROGER exits to kitchen with a shopping bag and ballons, then cleans up mess on kitchen counter.)*

BESS. She's having a party. She wants to string them up.

BESS. We never use the house. Why should we have Christmas lights?

DAVID. *(into phone)* No, I'm sorry, we don't have any. No, I don't think we have any balls either. We usually spend Christmas in New York.

BESS. Can she call back later? Your father is missing!

DAVID. *(into phone)* What? Well, uh ... I'm sure it's all right, but I'll ask. *(to BESS)* She wants to know if she can put red and green bulbs in all the lamps.

BESS. *(Takes the phone.)* Mrs. Dalcimer, do what you want. Have a nice party! *(Hangs up, abruptly.)* Ohhh, I just can't wait any longer. I've got to call the police.

DAVID. 444-1- *(ROGER re-enters and stands at kitchen arch.)*

SHELBY. David!

BESS. *(Picks up phone, dials 0)* Operator, ... get me the police.... *(DAVID throws up his hands in uselessness.)*

(As offstage we hear two men singing, "Take Me Out To The Ballgame." When they hear the singing, the kids laugh. ROGER crosses DR to armchair. SHELBY crosses D to sofa and lies on it, kicking off shoes. DAVID crosses R to bookcase. BESS starts to lower the phone. The front door opens to reveal LES and NATE MOODY, both drunk, [NATE well stoned] and singing. BESS, now angry, crosses L, to table.)

LES and NATE. *(Sing.)*
BUY ME SOME PEANUTS AND CRACKER JACKS
I DON'T CARE IF I NEVER GET BACK
SO LET'S ROOT ROOT ROOT FOR THE HOME TEAM
IF THEY DON'T WIN IT'S A SHAME
(They enter here.)
FOR IT'S ONE, TWO, THREE STRIKES YOU'RE OUT
AT THE OLD BALLL GAMMMMEE!

LES. *(Closes the door, the kids applaud.)* SPORTS FANS ... I'm home!

BESS. Oh, Les ... where have you been?

LES. I'm home! And I have brought a guest. I want you to meet Nate Moody. Nate, say a few words. *(NATE is unable to. He leans forward as if to speak, but nothing comes out.)* Very well put! *(LES helps NATE to lean on C railing.)*

BESS. Les, are you all right? I was worried.

LES. As they say in the trade, I'm golden...

BESS. Where did you go...? I almost called the police.. I

DAVID. We thought you were going to Houston.

LES. Did I say I was going to Houston?

BESS. That's what you said before you left.

LES. Ohhhh yes. Oh well. We didn't go. We didn't go, did we Nate? *(NATE shakes head "no.")*

LES. *(with his arm around NATE'S shoulder)* We went to Harrisburg. We went to Harrisburg. Did you know that Harrisburg is the state capital of Pennsylvania. We went to Harrisburg. We got on the wrong plane. When we landed I said to Nate, I said ... Gee .. Gee, we got to Houston quick! Harrisburg. You know, Harrisburg is no place to be late at night. Everybody is asleep. So, both of us, knowing it is the state capital of Pennsylvania, we went to take a look at the capitol. It's .. It's very similar to all other state capitols. You know .. white, and there's a dome, I think. I may be wrong. But.. Oh! *(Crosses D to C.)* And then we sang a song to the governor, and then we went down to the river. The Susquahanna runs right into town... We went down to the river and skipped stones. I got one to skip seven times! We had a ball. A veritable ball...

BESS. *(Sits at table, acts more annoyed than she really is.)* I was worried .. I called everywhere .. I

LES. Ahhhh *(Goes to her.)* I'm sorry... I should have called or something. But I was having such a wonderful time, I completely forgot! Hey! Listen, we almost went to Chicago! *(Crosses U to NATE, grabs him, lets go, NATE falls against US wall, streamers hang down almost in his face.)* Nate said Sandy Koufax is pitching tomorrow against the Cubs. We were gonna take a plane to Chicago. God, that's a great ball park. *(Crosses R, to DAVID.)* Old man Wrigley still knows how to play baseball. Only in the afternoon. And he's got those ivy covered walls out there. He's got crummy ball teams but one hell of a park!

BESS. Why don't.....

LES. *(staggering around at R)* There were no planes to Chicago. You had to go to New York first. I said, "That doesn't make sense. New York's the other way!" So we came back to New York. Well, I figured if I was in New York, I might as well come home. So herree I am! *(Crosses DR, then to sofa and tickles SHELBY'S feet.)*

BESS. I'll get you and Nate some coffee.... *(Exits to kitchen.)*

LES. *(Crosses UC.)* Thatsss a good idea. Nate? You want some coffee?

NATE. *(who has reached the railing again)* Wait'll we get to Chicago.

LES. OK! ..... uh ... boys ... I think he could use a chair. *(SHELBY crosses U to LES. ROGER and DAVID help NATE over to the couch. They sit him down. He gives ROGER a two dollar tip, which ROGER splits with DAVID.)*

NATE. I'd like a corner room. Over the lake please!

SHELBY. Dad ... are you all right?

LES. Nevah .. betta! *(ROGER and SHELBY meet USC. DAVID stands at R end of sofa.)*

BESS. *(Comes back with cup for LES.)* Why don't you come over to the table...?

LES. *(Turns toward the table and sees all the liquor bottles on the cabinet.)* What's all that???

DAVID. Oh, it's ours. We had a wedding party for Shelby.

LES. You drank up *all our liquor?*

DAVID. This isn't ours! It was BYO.

LES. A BYO wedding reception. That's ingenious!

BESS. David, clean it up! Please. *(SHELBY crosses to kitchen, gets cloth to wipe table and coffee pot for cabinet. ROGER strikes streamers and banner. DAVID gets 2 boxes and clears all the bottles from cabinet.)*

BESS. *(Leads LES to couch.)* Over here... *(He follows after her like a puppy dog as she puts coffee on coffee table in front of couch. NATE has passed out with his feet on the coffee table.)*

LES. Where are you taking me?

BESS. Sit. Drink your coffee. We have a show to do in twenty minutes.

LES. *(Leans, sips coffee.)* It's too hot.

BESS. Sit down and drink it, you'll burn yourself.

LES. I don't wanna sit down! I wanna stand up. I'm excited. If I sit down, all the excitement will .. will .. coagulate!

BESS. You've got to sober up before the show.

LES. I am sober! I'm just excited. *(He grabs her around the waist.)* It's been so long since you've seen me excited, you think I'm drunk! *(He dangerously steps over NATE'S legs which are propped up on the coffee table.)*

BESS. LES, we have a show to do! Will you sit down and drink your coffee???

LES. *(at fireplace, making a big show of not spilling his coffee)* NO! Not until you ask me why I went to Houston!!!

BESS. *(She sighs.)* Ohhh, God.

SHELBY. *(wiping table)* Why did you go to Houston?

(ROGER re-enters from kitchen, having taken off streamers, takes top box of bottles from DAVID, exits to kitchen.)

LES. I want your mother to ask me.

BESS. Children, I think we'd better be alone. It's going to be a *long* morning.

DAVID. She still calls us children. We're twenty years old!!! *(Exits to kitchen with box of bottles.)*

BESS. But you are still our children. Even when you are forty, you will still be "our children."

SHELBY. I hope not.

BESS. Now, would you all leave us alone.... I think you father and I have to talk.

SHELBY. I wanna know why he went to Houston.

(ROGER and DAVID re-enter. ROGER stands at kitchen arch. DAVID crosses to C, above the sofa.)

LES. I got a job offer.

SHELBY. *(Stops wiping.)* You did??? Are you going to take it??

LES. It depends on your mother.

SHELBY. *(CS)* Oh, Mom. Take it! Texas is terrific! Did you see *Giant*? You could have a big house like Rock Hudson and Liz Taylor. Out in the middle of nowhere. And David could have a big Caddy convertible and drive for miles and miles and miles and never hit anything! *(DAVID exits, DSR arch.)*

BESS. Shelby .. *please.*

ROGER. *(Crosses in to SHELBY.)* I think your Mom wants to be alone with your Dad. *(SHELBY nods .. as ROGER escorts her off. They exit thru USR arch and into her bedroom.)*

BESS. I'm beginning to really like that boy. *(Crosses L, to table.)*

LES. What boy?

BESS. *(Picks up cloth on table.)* Roger!

LES. Roger? .... Oh .. Roger. Yes ... Rog. How about Nate? Should I take him to the bedroom? *(Crosses to NATE, R of sofa.)*

BESS. *(Tosses cloth into kitchen.)* Forget about Nate. What is this about a job offer??

LES. *(Still holding coffee cup.)* Got your attention, eh??

BESS. Les!

LES. Wellll, while you were at the party, nob hobbing ... hobnoobing .. with...

BESS. Could you get to the point? We go on .. in 18 minutes.

LES. I'm getting to the point! If I just give you the point, you won't get it. So I'm *getting* to the point. The part that I'm telling you now *is* the getting. OK?

BESS. *(CS, leaning against table)* OK.

LES. *(Crosses U, above sofa.)* OK. Whillle you were talking to fortunate five hundred at the party .. I ... just happened to be talking to a man named Russell Darlington. Now, Mr. Darlington .. I was calling him "Russ" before long.... Well, "Russ," it just so happens, is one of the major investors in the new Houston Texas baseball team! *(Crosses to C, near Bess.)* Get it???

BESS. Not yet.

LES. Good. There's more. Y'see .. there's going to be a new major league team in Houston next year. The Houston .. the Houston... What the hell is the name of the team? *(Moves to NATE.)* Nate? What's the name of the new Houston team? *(As soon as NATE hears his name he wakes up, sits up and tries to act sober.)*

BESS. It doesn't matter.

LES. NATE, what's the name of the new Houston team??

BESS. Les, I don't care!

NATE. *(blurts it out)* Colt 45's.

LES. The Colt 45's. *(BESS shakes her head.)* I just want to give you all the details so you won't think I'm making this up.

BESS. *(checking watch)* I don't think you're making it up, but I wish you'd hurry.

LES. OK. The Houston Colt 45's. *(to NATE who is trying to stay awake)* Unfortunate name for a baseball team, but what the hell. I mean, if they wanted something Western, they could've called them the Stallions .. or the Long Horns, or the...

BESS. Les! *(NATE drops off again.)*

LES. *(CS)* OK. OK. Sooooo we started talking about the new ball team. Gonna be in the National League. Well, he didn't hear my name right off .. but ... he knew Nate. *(NATE wakes up, then drops off.)* Nate introduced us .. and he said ... are you the same Les Dischener who used to broadcast the old Brownies' games in St. Louis? I said, yes. He said ... Gol darn .. just like that .. Gol darn. I used to listen to you when I was a kid! He was a bit younger than me. *(Sits on L arm of sofa, puts cup down.)* One of those rich young Texans. But obviously he'd grown up in St. Louis. And he'd remembered me! And....

BESS. Les, we have fifteen minutes. *(Sits at table.)*

LES. I'm closing fast. And .... he says to me .. You know, we haven;t got any announcers picked yet for our broadcasts. Would you be interested? Welll, I said ... I don't

know... It's been a long time since I broadcast a game ..
but... He said .. c'mere. And he takes me and Nate into the
bathroom... *(NATE wakes up as LES crosses U and around to R
of sofa.)* ...and he says ... just give me a little bit of an old
Brownies game. And this guy, Russ, .. he sits down on the
john ... and closes his eyes .. and I put my hand over my
mouth, so I sounded like I was on the air, and I just said ...
"Stepping in now ... leading off for the Brownies .... number 6 .... Roy Seivers." *(NATE cups his hands around his mouth
and makes a breathy "crowd cheering" sound.)* The guy flipped.
He loved it. He's jumpin up and down in the bathroom...
shaking my hand. Yelling at me... "You gotta take this job
... You gotta do the Houston games." Well, I said ... I'm
interested, I'm interested. *(BESS checks her watch. NATE
nods off again.)* So... *(LES crosses UR, above sofa.)* He tells me
he's going to call his friend, Rip Rusher. These guys have
names. Rusher is the club prez. So he calls ol Rip and sets
up an appointment for me to see him tomorrow night for
dinner in Houston! He told me just to go down and toss a
few with old Rip. *(Crosses to C.)* As far as he was concerned,
I had it made! What the hell, I was excited. I grabbed
Nate. *(NATE wakes up, then nods off.)* I said, why wait till
tomorrow. Let's go tonight! So we went out to the airport
and .... well, you know the rest.

BESS. Harrisburg.

LES. Right. *(BESS nods.)* What do you think?

BESS. I think we'd better get things ready for the program. *(She gets up, crosses L, to cabinet.)*

LES. Do you think I should take the job?

BESS. *(She sighs, looks away.)* Do you *have* the job?

LES. Not yet. But I will...

BESS. I'll discuss it with you when you have it.

LES. I don't want to go down there if I know you won't come.

BESS. *(Sets up equipment, the console, mike, and phone and plugs everything in.)* I don't wanna discuss it if you don't have the job.

LES. I have it. It's 99 percent sure.

BESS. Like the restaurant. You were *sure* that would succeed.

LES. That was *your* idea. You said open a restaurant. I didn't want to run a restaurant. I hate restaurants. They're full of people. Eating! Did you ever stand and watch people eat for six hours a night? My heart wasn't in it. *(Sits on L arm of sofa.)*

BESS.   BESS. How about the musical? You *loved* that show. That was your idea.

LES. Yes it was, but we lost our star and our director had a nervous breakdown.

BESS. That hasn't stopped other hits! No one wanted to see a musical about the Norsemen.

LES. Why not? They go to shows about leprechauns, gangsters, Siamese kings ... why not Norsemen?

BESS. *(Crosses C, next to him — dead-pan, straight out.)* The opening song should have clued you in. "Oh ho, we are the Norsemen/Oh ho we always stay on course men!" *(Rolls her eyes, crosses U, to front door, gets newspapers from hall.)*

LES. You had to pick the one lousy lyric.

BESS. That was a good one. *(Closes door, crosses to desk.)*

LES. The music was terrific!

BESS. *(Puts papers down on desk.)* Then why did it fail?

LES. The critics hated it. What did they know?

BESS. *(Lifts out section with column.)* More than you did. You're a sports writer, Les. Why don't you stick to that?

LES. *(Crosses DR, then UC to her.)* I have tried. There is no work here. Newspapers are folding left and right. The Dodgers left. The Giants left. People are leaving New York, Bess. The country is growing. There are intelligent, interesting people everywhere now. I hear Los Angeles has a French restaurant!

BESS. You could find work here. You could write your book!

LES. I'm trying. It's not something you just sit down and do every day.

BESS. Writers do!

LES. Well. I'm... It's a different kind of writing. *(Crosses D, to sofa.)* I'm used to short pieces. I'm used to a deadline! Maybe if I had a little... *(Sits next to the sleeping NATE.)*

BESS. How about "The Book They Said I'd Never Write."

LES. That's a low blow.

BESS. *(Slams newspaper down on desk.)* Blaming the show for everything that's gone wrong in your life is a lower blow. Blaming my success for your failure is the lowest blow of all. *(Crosses DC.)*

LES. I never did that.

BESS. You're doing it now. Asking me to give this all up and move to Texas. What do you call that? *(Leans against table.)*

LES. I call that asking you to start over with me. *(leaning on sofa arm, toward her)* Bess! My beeaautiful Bess. My lovely

Bess. Remember how much fun it was when I was a hardworking sports columnist and you were a gung ho political reporter? If that damn gossip columnist on the News hadn't gotten sick, you'd probably have six Pulitzer Prizes by now. Whatever you do, you do well. You got a job to write schlock and you wrote schlock so well .. you're still writing it. And we've been broadcasting it for ten years! But, Bess .. this is our opportunity. We can go back. We can .. we can .. erase all the success that has made us so miserable and go back and be excited about our work again. *(She stands there silently. He moves to her.)* Remember how excited we were? Remember the breakfast we had with Mayor LaGuardia .. when he thanked you for dogging him about the Harlem Housing Projects. That was exciting. *(BESS crosses U, to desk. LES crosses DR.)* Remember when we flew to Chicago in '48 to watch the Eagles-Cardinals football final in the blinding snowstorm? With one-eyed Tommy Thompson .. the Eagles Quarterback .. trying to find his receivers .. and we're sitting there in the stands with our hands in hot chocolate! We were excited about everything. And each other. *(BESS crosses D to table with her folders.)* Look at us now. You are the world's busiest woman. I am the world's most unmotivated man. *(He moves CS, back to her now.)* Look... I've got a proposal. I'll... I'll go to Texas... I'll take this job. You come down .. for awhile. Take a leave of absence. You could do that. Just look the place over. You'll probably love it. I mean .. we could get some .. adobe house out in the desert. You'd have a place out in the sun to sit and work on that book *you* always wanted to write ... about America's crazy love affair with celebrities ... what was that ... "American

Royalty"... *(BESS sits C chair.)* You used to talk about that book all the time.. that was a great idea.. so.. you could sit out there at a nice ... big picnic table.. and I'd come home from the ball games .. and cook up a barbeque dinner.. *(He sits on L arm of sofa.)* ...and we'd have friends over ... two or three friends, like normal people ... and we'd sit out late ... and look up at that sky .. and talk ... and .. do all the dumb things ordinary people do. We've tried everything else. Let's try this! *(His voice cracks a little, Teary-eyed.)* I loved you once .. and you were nuts about me... We wanted to be important writers. And we loved that dream. You know what we are now? Famous. We're famous. That's *all.* We're lousy parents. Lousy, lousy lovers, but *famous....* *(There is a long pause as he looks at her. She shows no signs of response.)*

(Studio phone buzzes and lights up. BESS picks it up.)

BESS. *(into phone)* Yes ... yes ... all set. OK .... right. Fine. *(Hangs up.)* Five minutes. *(into mike)* Good morning, one, two, three, four. *(She looks thru her notes.)*

LES. *(Picks up his coffee cup, walks slowly to the table, removing his tie. He sits.)* You know what my fondest wish is? That one day .. we could have a long ... lovely .. easy talk .. without this thing *(microphone)* between us..... *(BESS ignores that, is going thru last minute papers as LES looks up, then suddenly, he stands, unplugs the microphone, puts it into the cabinet, shuts the cabinet, locks it, takes key.)*

BESS. Wh — what are you doing?

LES. I'm taking the bull by the horns. No show today! No more show! We are going off! *(Crosses UC toward door.)*

BESS. *(rises)* Les, give me that key.

LES. *(He backs away.)* Nope, no more show.

BESS. *(Runs USR.)* Please...

LES. *(Opens front door, goes out into hall.)* No show today! *(like town crier)* No show today!

BESS. *(Turns and shouts to the bedrooms.)* David! Roger! Come here!

LES. *(Re-enters, closes the door.)* All ya havta do is just take a little trip to Texas. You're gonna love it. Comme on. I'm flying down there this afternoon. I'm having dinner with this guy tonight. He'd love to see you. You'd love it there. Lyndon Johnson has a ranch down there!

BESS. He deserves it.

LES. Come on..... *(Crosses DL.)*

BESS. *(stepping USC)* DAVID! *(to LES)* Les, enough is enough.

LES. That's what I've been saying. Enough is enough. *(Sits at table with feet up on table, dangling key at BESS.)*

(DAVID, in pajamas, still wearing girl's hat, ROGER, in bathrobe, SHELBY, in a towel and slippers, enter.)

DAVID. *(at USR arch)* What's the matter?

SHELBY. *(at bookcase with ROGER DS of her)* What's wrong?

BESS. *(Crosses to DAVID.)* Your father has locked the cabinet, turned off the equipment. We go on in a few minutes. Will you get the key from him?

DAVID. Why?

BESS. Because I can't go on the air without it!

DAVID. Then I think you shouldn't go on.

BESS. That is none of your business! Get the key.

DAVID. If it's none of my business, then why should I get the key? *(LES blows his son an appreciative kiss.)*

BESS. *(Crosses d, to ROGER, pushes him CS.)* Oh God .. Roger .. would you please get the key from Mr. Dischenger?

SHELBY. Don't get Roger in the middle of this.

BESS. You stay out of it! Roger ... this is an emergency. Our show goes on in .. *(checks)* Oh God .. two minutes... Would you be so kind as to wrench the key from Mr. Dischenger so we can go on the air.

ROGER. *(Looks at LES, who puts up his "dukes.")* Well, Mam ... I haven't been in the family very long.

BESS. This is not a family matter. This is a military matter. Get that key!

ROGER. Shelby ... what do I do?

SHELBY. I think you should stay out of it.

BESS. If he stays out of it, he's helping your father!! Ohhhhh. *(She starts L for LES, as ROGER gets out of her way and crosses R to SHELBY at bookcase.)*

LES. *(Rises, runs DS and up around the table, blocks BESS' path with a chair.)* And now, ladies and gentlemen, here we are at Churchill Downs .. where Mrs. Bess Dischenger is breaking out of the gate— *(BESS proceeds to stalk LES around the room as LES backs away. DSR, the kids watch. David, watching SHELBY, to insure the continuance of the chase.)* It's two minutes to .. Bess, old girl, .. you'd better hurry. *(DAVID "plays" his cheeks, making horse-trotting noises.)*

BESS. *(at L of sofa, removing her high-heel shoes)* Les... I'll........ I'lll...... So help me...

LES. You'll what...? *(BESS starts to run at him. He crosses U

above sofa and around back to DSR) Ladies and gentlemen...
it's a beautiful dripping day ... and Mrs. Dischenger is
now circling the couch .. now moving around down the
straightaway .. here she comes ... beautiful stride ...
beautiful...

BESS. Les, I beg you.... *(DAVID, who is UC holds up his
hands, LES tosses him the key. DAVID now dangles the key. BESS
runs US at him as he tosses the key back to LES.)*

BESS. *(to DAVID)* You rat! *(NATE wakes up and looks
around, puzzled. BESS makes quick move to LES, DR. He retreats.
DS and then U the C steps.)*

LES. Oh ... a sudden burst ... a sudden burst of power
from the lovely filly ... and she's moved to the three-
quarter post ... down the rug ... past the coffee table and
up the steps ... it's a beautiful race..... *(As they run past
DAVID, he leaps over the railing to the lower level.)*

BESS. Les, for God's sake... *(chasing him U and out the
USR arch)*

LES. *(Runs in thru DSR arch, BESS in pursuit.)* A beautiful
race and ... here she comes ... around the final turn and
into the homestretch.... *(BESS follows him, as he runs between
the sofa and the credenza, past railing, over which DAVID has lept
again, to the upper level.)* Right on the rail ... hugging the rail
... into the stretch... *(BESS follows him L around the table
again, then across to C. Out of breath, she leans against the C railing.)* Charging in toward the finish line .. charging .. charging ... charging... *(LES runs U to the windows above the desk.)*
Charging.... *(BESS feebly reaches out for him. LES sweeps his
arm around and "throws" key out window, then crosses D to the C of
the railing, right above BESS.)* Ahhhhh, too bad ... she lost!
(They look at each other, breathing hard. BESS slaps him. She

moves toward cabinet. She hastens as she picks up letter-opener from the desk and, kneeling on the floor, begins to pry cabinet open.)

BESS. David ... David .. come help me with this ... DAVID.

(NATE goes back to sleep.)

DAVID. Come on, Mom.....

SHELBY. *(Crosses L, toward cabinet.)* David ... for God's sake ... Roger ... enough..... Will you please help my mother open the cabinet....?

ROGER. *(Still at bookcase, looks to LES.)* Sir?

SHELBY. Roger, please ... *I'm* asking you.

LES. Better go..... *(ROGER starts to cross to BESS, frantically trying to pry open cabinet.)* Roger! *(ROGER stops, turns. LES holds out key.)* Use this.... *(Tosses him the key.)*

BESS. *(rises)* Hurry up ... hurry..... *(ROGER crosses DL and opens cabinet.)*

LES. *(checking watch)* She might make it ... Yes... *(BESS takes out mike, turns on things, with ROGER helping. She kneels and checks the connections on the floor. ROGER helps her.)* Right now, in Passaic, New Jersey,................Mrs. Murphy is just now poaching her husband's egg and Mr. Murphy is wandering, glassy-eyed into his kitchen *(LES crosses DR, heads L, to table.)* ..and looking at his ugly wife as she turns from his egg and switches on the radio ... and now.. as the radio warms up.. *(BESS crosses to credenza for more papers in drawer. SHELBY moves away R.)* ..Mr. Murphy moves to his wife and tenderly kisses her warm cheek with his cold mouth .. turns .. scratches himself .. and sits down. "Here's your egg," she says.. "Now shuddup, Les and Bess is on"....

(Yellow warning light flashes. LESS flicks on the monitor switch and stands DSL.)

RADIO. It's 8:05 and time for Breakfast with Les and Bess, with Bess Christen and Les Dischinger. *(Continues under rest.)*

(Studio phone buzzes, BESS is busy, getting papers organized for show. Phone buzzes again.)

BESS. *(Motions to ROGER, who is USL.)* Get that! Roger, pick up the phone.

ROGER. *(Sits at table and picks up phone. Into phone.)* Hello. Yes...?? *(to BESS)* Drop the Madison Furs Commercial.

BESS. What?

ROGER. Kill the furs!

RADIO. So let's go up to their cozy apartment, here in Manhattan.

BESS. Tell them it's OK.

ROGER. *(into phone)* It's OK.

RADIO. ...and have some breakfast!

(LES is at table now. Red "on air" light goes on.)

BESS. *(Staggers to table, flicks off monitor switch.)* Good morning, darling.

LES. *(sooo cheerful)* Good morning dear.

ROGER. *(still on phone)* I'm not David.... I'm just a guest here. *(BESS gives him a cold stare.)*

ROGER. *(quickly)* Bye. *(He hangs up, starts to retreat. BESS shakes her head, distressed at that having gone out. LES puts his arm around ROGER, keeping him at the table. They stand UL of table. BESS sinks into her chair, still out of breath.)*

LES. *(He's definitely still a little drunk.)* Wellll, did we go to a wonderful party last night. It was our annual blast for the refugee parents and even though I was only there for about half of it ... it was as good a half a party as I've been to in a long time. Wouldn't you say so, dear?

BESS. Uh ... yes.. It...

LES. BUT, before we give you allll the details about the party, we have a bit of special news of our own. Our lovely daughter, Shelby, who you've met many times on the program, came home yesterday with her very own Ensign! She went off and got married! How about saying hello, Shelb?

SHELBY. *(at end table, R.)* Da-ad.....

LES. Ensign, maybe you'd like to say a few words. Roger, this is Roger... *(LES obviously can't remember. ROGER says "EVERSON." BESS is mortified. LES repeats the name.)* ...Everson, from Utah. I'm not sure we can be heard in Utah ... but who knows .... Roger....

ROGER. Uh.....

BESS. *(loud whisper)* You don't *have* to.

ROGER. Well.....

LES. Come on.... It's a family tradition. Ask Shelby and David. They were on the program for every major event in their lives. I remember the day David got his braces on his teeth. His description of that was one of radio's finest hours!

DAVID. *(UC of railing)* I could tell it **again**! *(Crosses DL to table.)*

LES. *(Laughs and pulls up another chair.)* OK. Come on Roger. Just a hello to your mom, at least. *(LES sits in SL chair.)*

ROGER. *(Comes reluctantly, and sits with DAVID, standing behind him.)* Well ... uh ... hello Mom.

LES. You want to tell everyone what you do?

ROGER. I'm an Ensign in the United States Navy.

LES. Anything else?

ROGER. I'm a Mormon. *(Everyone does a shocked "take.")*

LES. No kidding? Hey, Shelb .. did you know that?

SHELBY. *(embarrassed)* Da-ad.

LES. You don't have any other wives, do you?

ROGER. No sir! *(SHELBY mimes a "phew!")*

LES. Well, I know all our listeners wish you and Shelby the best of luck and health and happiness. Now listen .. *don't* send any presents. We got a lot of presents when Shelby was in the hospital for her appendectomy. And they were wonderful .. but these kids don't need anything.

BESS. *(recovering)* Maybe they could send a contribution to the Refugee Children's Fund.

LES. Those kids don't need anything either!

BESS. Well.....

DAVID. How about the N double A C P!

LES. David suggests the N double A CP! Do we have any other suggestions?

DAVID. How about the American Civil Liberties Union?

LES. David also suggests the American Civil Liberties Union.

DAVID. *(Comes to mike, leans in.)* I think, since she's

married a military man, it should go to some non-military cause!

BESS. *(pushing DAVID back)* I think we should talk about last night's party!

LES. Good idea! Y'know, we were the hit of that party!

BESS. Well, I wouldn't say that.

LES. Yes we were. We sang a song.

BESS. Oh, that.

LES. What do you mean, "Oh, that." We were terrific! Would you like to hear it?

BESS. Les ... be serious.

SHELBY. Yes! Oh, Mom .. come on.

LES. Let me see if I have it... *(Searches inside coat pocket for paper.)* Yes! Here it is.

DAVID. It's not one of Sarah Winfield's famous parodies?

LES. It most certainly is!

DAVID. I vote for hearing it!

BESS. No—not on the air.

LES. Now you folks out there have *never* heard us do one of our famous Sarah Winfield parodies. You've been faithful all these years... I think it's about time....

BESS. Les, no...........

SHELBY. *(Crosses in to US of BESS, stands next to ROGER.)* Come on, Mom!

LES. OK ... Now ... now you have to picture this. The room was filled with people. New York's finest! People who were used to nothing less than vintage Cole Porter... and Bess comes out in a little coolie hat, representing a Korean foster child. *(LES grabs a folder and opens it on BESS'S head.)*

BESS. Thank you.

LES. You're welcome! And I'm in some kind of.... *(DAVID gives him lady's hat.)*

LES. Thank you. ...hat representing a Hungarian or Greek or something....

BESS. *(warming up)* And Sarah Winfield was at the piano...

LES. Representing the death of the American Musical Theater.

BESS. And the whole party stopped. The whole party. And everyone sat and Mindy MoscoKowitz came out .. she's the Bonwit's heir .. and said .. We have a treat... Two of our darling children are here tonight to entertain you....

LES. And out we came. Ready? .. one .. two .. three...

LES and BESS. *(Sing to the tune of "Because of You.*")*

BECAUSE OF YOU, WE HAVE THREE MEALS A DAY

BECAUSE OF YOU, WE CAN LAUGH, WE CAN PLAY

BECAUSE OF YOU, WE CAN GO TO SCHOOL

AND THERE WE LEARN THE GOLDEN RULE

TO BE KIND, LIKE YOU'RE KIND TO US.

BECAUSE OF YOU, WE HAVE GOOD CLOTHES TO WEAR

BECAUSE OF YOU, WE HAVE PEOPLE WHO CARE

*License to produce BREAKFAST WITH LES AND BESS does *not include* the right to use this song.

BECAUSE OF YOU
OUR LIVES ARE NOW WORTHWHILE
AND WE CAN SMILE
BECAUSE OF YOU.

Les. *(Sings.)*
SO PLEASE KEEP WRITING...

Both. *(Sing.)*
AND WE CAN SMILE BECAUSE OF YOU

Les. *(Sings.)*
AND SEND MORE MOOLAH...

Both. *(Sing.)*
AND WE CAN SMILE BECAUSE OF YOUUUU!!!
(They laugh and the kids clap. ROGER, a bit bewildered, applauds too.)

Les. *(grinning)* Well ... we didn't do badly, did we? Singing *to-geth-er!*

Bess. *(Smiling in spite of herself, shakes her head.)* No ... it was .. really quite fun .. the party...

Les. I have something else we can do together. Something we can all do together.

Bess. *(anxious)* What?

Les. We haven't all been together on the show for a long time. And in honor of Shelby's marriage, I think we all ought to play a little game we used to play when the kids were kids... And, you, there at home eating your little eggs, .. you can play too.

Bess. Les... I think, maybe...

Les. The game is called, Yeah-Boo.

Bess. Now, Les, we had the song...

Les. And it's easy to play... I'm going to tell a story .. and when I say something you like ... you say Yeah ... and

when I say something you don't like, you say Boooo ..
OK?

BESS. Les, maybe we can play some other time ... I
think....

LES. I think this is a perfect time. Look who we got
here: .. Shelby ... David ... Roger ... you ready...?

DAVID. *(loudly)* Yeahhhhh.

LES. Shelby ... Roger...?

SHELBY. *(giggling)* We hear you, Dad....

LES. OK, join in now... Nate, you too. That's right. I
forgot to tell you. My old friend, Nate Moody, is here.
Nate? *(DAVID crosses R and nudges him awake.)*

NATE. *(sitting up)* I'll have a BLT and a coke.

BESS. Les.... *(DAVID helps NATE up, with difficulty, and
they stagger toward the table.)*

LES. It's all right .. I think this'll be fun ... ready ... Yeah
.. boo... If the kids haven't gone off to school ... stop 'em,
bring 'em back and let them play too... Here we go... Now
.. "We're gonna open a bar..."

DAVID and NATE. *(NATE'S response over-shadows DAVID.)*
Yeahhhhh.

LES. *(laughing)* Come on, let's hear it. "We're gonna
open a bar..."

DAVID, LES and NATE. Yeahhhhhhhhhhh.

LES. Come on, Shelby ... Roger ... really come on....

DAVID. Go on, Shelby...

SHELBY and ROGER. *(a bit timid)* Yeahhhhh.

LES. Good. But ... there's gonna be a lock on the
door...

DAVID, LES, SHELBY and NATE. Boooooooooo.

LES. But everybody has a key!

DAVID, LES, SHELBY and NATE. *(really enjoying the game)* Yeahhhhhhhh!

LES. Only it doesn't fit.....

ALL. *(All now join but BESS, who is quite disturbed.)* Boooooooo!

LES. So we saw off the lock.

ALL. Yeahhhhhhh!

LES. But the door is jammed!

ALL. Boooooo!

LES. So we knock it down!

ALL. Yeahhhhhhh!

LES. But there's nothing in the bar!

ALL. Booooooooo!

LES. Except beer barrels....

ALL. Yeahhhhhhh!

LES. But we don't know how to open them.

ALL. Boooooo!

LES. They're open.....

ALL. Yeahhhhhhhaaaa!

LES. But there's no glasses ... to drink it with....

ALL. Booooooo!

LES. Just pitchers.....

ALL. Yeaaaaaaaa!

LES. But the pitchers have a hole in them....

ALL. Booooo!

LES. At the top.....

ALL. Yeahhhhhh!

LES. But it really isn't beer.....

ALL. Boooooo!

LES. It's scotch....

ALL. Yeaaaaaaaaaaaa!

LES. But we finish it all....

ALL. Booooooo!

LES. But there's more at home.....

ALL. Yeahhhhh!

LES. But so is the wife.....

ALL. Booooooo!

LES. But she's pretty.....

ALL. Yeaaaaaaa!

LES. She's pretty angry.....

ALL. Booooooo!

LES. She's pretty angry.. when you tell her about all the great new plans you have.

ALL. Yeahhh!

LES. And she tells you you're drunk and your plans are ridiculous.

ALL. Boooo!

BESS. *(It's going too far, she's getting upset.)* Les ... Les ... please.. *(Grabs for cough button, he pulls it away.)*

LES. And you tell her you're not drunk. You're excited. And your plans are exciting.

DAVID, LES and NATE. Yeahhhh!

BESS. *(She crosses to CS, pleading with him to stop.)* Les!

LES. But she tells you to forget about your excitement so she can do her idiotic radio program for the Murphy's in Passaic.

LES, DAVID and NATE. Boooooo!

BESS. *(Rises out of mike range.)* Les .... please. Please, please, please, please. Please.

(The studio phone is flashing.)

(The studio phone is flashing.)

LES. And you tell her to get the hell off the air anyway and come to Texas and make something out of the marriage.

BESS. Les. *(She picks up the studio phone and crosses R with it to coffee table, turning her back to them.)*

LES, DAVID and NATE. Yeaaaaaaaaaaa!

SHELBY. *(Crosses to C.)* David. Daddy. Please. Daddy!

(Red light goes off.)

LES. But she won't do it.

LES, DAVID and NATE. Boooooooo!

LES. She has an obligation to the Murphys ... the millions of Murphys...

LES, DAVID and NATE. Yeaaaaaaaa!

LES. And she won't do it.........

ALL. Booooooo!

BESS. *(Hangs up, stunned.)* They cut us off! Les, they cut us off! *(ROGER crosses to SHELBY in the C.)*

LES. They cut us off!!

LES, DAVID and NATE. Yeaaaaaaaaa!

BESS. *(getting angry now)* You know what's going to happen now? Steiner's going to call.

LES. Steiner will call.....

LES, DAVID and NATE. Booooooo.

BESS. *(Crosses in, to table.)* He's going to use this to cancel us. That will be all. That will be all.

LES. That will be all.

LES, DAVID and NATE. Yeaaaaaaa.

BESS. *(Crosses DR, paces.)* Unless I can save it.

LES. Booooo! *(NATE distracts DAVID, but all eyes are on BESS.)*

BESS. Unless I can tell him you're "sick," and I'm having nothing more to do with you. I'll do it alone.

LES. Booooo!

BESS. *(almost screaming)* You want to go to Texas, go. Go. See if I care. I don't need you, Les. I can do this alone. I can do it *all* without you! *(She storms off thru DSR arch and up into her bedroom, slams door. ROGER, SHELBY and DAVID watch LES as he stares after BESS.)*

LES. Booooooo! Booooooooo! Booooooooo! Booooooo! Booooooo! Booooooo!

(As Curtain Falls)

ACT TWO

Scene 2

Time: Early following morning.

Set: Living room.

As lights come up, ROGER sits on sofa, surrounded by suitcases, reading a copy of **Anna Karenina.** *He checks his watch, looks toward bedroom, sighs. SHELBY enters from DR arch, carrying a large shopping bag, which she places up near the front door.*

ROGER. *(Rises, crosses R.)* What's that for??
SHELBY. It's got my quilt in it.
ROGER. What do you need your quilt for? I have blankets in Norfolk.
SHELBY. *(Crosses DC.)* I want something of my own! I'm gonna be in a strange town in a strange apartment, seeing nothing but strangers... I wanna have something familiar!
ROGER. I'm familiar!
SHELBY. *(Crosses L, into kitchen.)* You're gonna be at sea a lot!

ROGER. *(Sighs, puts book down on credenza, puts on hat, picks up 2 suitcases, SR.)* All right .. let's go!

SHELBY. *(Enters with bowl of cereal and bottle of milk, sits at table.)* I still think we ought to say goodbye to Mom.

ROGER. *(Crosses C, to her with suitcases in hands.)* If we say goodbye to your mother, we'll never get out of here.

SHELBY. It's not polite.

ROGER. Who's polite around here???

SHELBY. *(rises)* Calm down ... we'll go in a minute. *(She starts off, DSR.)*

ROGER. What are you getting now?

SHELBY. My pillow.

ROGER. I have pillows!

SHELBY. Do you have one with Cinderella embroidered on it? *(She exits. He takes the 2 suitcases up to the door as:)*

(Front door opens and DAVID enters.)

DAVID. Heyyyy! *(Sees suitcases.)* Going somewhere??

ROGER. We're going to Norfolk.

DAVID. God, why???

ROGER. *(Puts down suitcases.)* I'm stationed there!

DAVID. Shelby has to go too?

ROGER. Of course.

DAVID. Does she know that???

ROGER. Of course. We're married! *(Crosses DC, picks up other 3 suitcases.)*

SHELBY. *(Enters from DR with pillow, crosses UC to DAVID.)* You're home! Where were you??

DAVID. *(Crosses D, puts school books on table.)* Jeff Pozner had an all-night exam-studying party.

SHELBY. *(following him)* Did you study?

DAVID. At the beginning. Then we decided we're all gonna move to Los Angeles and start a rock and roll band! *(Exits to kitchen.)*

ROGER. *(Crosses U to door with suitcases.)* Shelby, let's go!!

SHELBY. *(Crosses U to ROGER at door.)* Mom's up. I hear her in the bathroom. Just let's say goodbye! Maybe Dad'll be back and we can say goodbye to him? *(ROGER shakes his head, manages to pick up all 5 suitcases.)*

DAVID. *(Enters with small box of cornflakes, sits on L chair at table.)* Where's Dad?

SHELBY. *(Crosses D to table, sits on C chair.)* He went to Houston, dummy! About that job!

DAVID. Norfolk. Houston. Los Angeles. There's not gonna be anybody left in this town but Mom.

(BESS enters from USR arch, goes to front door, gets newspapers. ROGER jockeys with suitcases to try to get out of door but as he is about to, BESS closes it.)

BESS. Good morning. What's going on here?

SHELBY. We're just about to leave. We wanted to say goodbye.

BESS. Leave???? Where are you going?? *(Crosses DC to SHELBY.)*

SHELBY. *(rises)* To Norfolk. I told you that.

BESS. No you didn't! I thought you were going to live here.

SHELBY. I can't live here!

BESS. Why, is it against regulations?

SHELBY. I have to live with Roger!

BESS. Roger lives on a ship!

SHELBY. Not all the time!

BESS. *(Drops newspapers on sofa.)* Where does he live the rest of the time?

SHELBY. At the Naval base in Norfolk.

BESS. You're going to live in a barracks?

(ROGER puts down the suitcases.)

SHELBY. They have apartments.

BESS. Like ours?

SHELBY. Oh, mother. I'm going to be *fine*! I've got my quilt and my Cinderella pillow!

ROGER. *(Crosses DC, between them.)* Mam, we've got a plane to catch .. so, if you don't mind.

BESS. Couldn't you stay just another day? We wanted to take you out to dinner. Celebrate. Get to know Roger. Roger, I hardly know you.

ROGER. It's all right, Mam.

BESS. *(Crosses DR.)* My daughter going off with a man I hardly know .. to live is some barracks in Virginia. You could certainly wait one more day!

ROGER. My ship sails in three days, Mam. We need to leave today.

BESS. I could call the Secretary of the Navy. I'm sure....

DAVID. Hey, Mom! You're not getting the message. They *want* to go! *(Takes a swig of milk from the bottle.)*

BESS. No one asked you!

ROGER. We're going to be late.... *(He leads SHELBY U to the suitcases, picks them up again.)*

DAVID. *(Runs UC.)* No sweat. I'll get you there.

BESS. You're not driving them anywhere.

DAVID. *(coming D to steps, C)* Why not?

BESS. Your license has been revoked. You're not allowed to drive.

DAVID. I'm only driving them to the airport. You know how many thousands of cars are going to the airport right now? Do you know what the chances are of my being stopped?

BESS. One hundred percent!

SHELBY. We'll take a cab. You can help us down with the bags. *(DAVID shrugs as SHELBY hands him the shopping bag and her make-up case. He exits. ROGER stands at door, impatiently, with the 5 other cases. Still holding her pillow, SHELBY crosses DR to BESS.)* I'll call you from down there. *(SHELBY hugs BESS and runs back up to the door. BESS turns away, teary.)* Mom ... you all right? *(BESS doesn't move.)* Mom? *(BESS starts to cry and crosses to the table, sits on C chair. SHELBY looks back at the anxious ROGER.)* Find a cab, I'll be right down.

ROGER. Shel-by!

SHELBY. *(Goes to ROGER.)* I'll be right there. *(Loads the pillow on top of the suitcases in his arms, kisses him. ROGER, struggling with the luggage, exits. SHELBY closes the door and crosses DC.)* Mom ... you can't do this to me. When I wanted to go to camp one summer, you cried and I stayed home. When I wanted to go to Europe one summer, you cried and I sayed home. I know underprivileged kids who have traveled more than I have!

BESS. I'm sorry.

SHELBY. It's not that you like having me here, you just hate to see me go!

BESS. I love having you here.

SHELBY. We never see each other. We never talk. You just panic when I leave. Well, I can't take it. I've got a husband and a whole new life now. I've got someone who really cares about me. I'm going to live with him. *(Crosses UC, above railing.)*

BESS. You're not going to see him either. He works on a boat!

SHELBY. A ship!

BESS. *(rises)* A boat. A ship. Why didn't you find a man who would be with you all the time?

SHELBY. Well, I don't think I'm ready for *that* kind of a marriage.

BESS. Ohhhh, God. We're all hopeless. It's hereditary. *(She goes US and embraces SHELBY.)* What are we gonna do?

SHELBY. I'm gonna go off and try to be happy.

BESS. And leave me here alone.

SHELBY. MOM!

BESS. *(Crosses DC, sighs.)* Your father called late last night. They made him an offer. To broadcast the games .. starting next year. And he can start working there now .. doing PR for the team.

SHELBY. Did he take it?

BESS. He's going to sleep on it. *(Crosses DR.)* What's there to sleep on? He knows he wants the job. Why doesn't he tell me and get it over with.

SHELBY. Maybe he thinks you're not ready to hear it.

BESS. I'm ready to hear it. I'm just not ready for him to leave!

SHELBY. *(Crosses DC.)* Why don't you give up the show? Go to Texas.

BESS. I'm not ready to do that.

SHELBY. *(Steps to L of sofa.)* What are you ready for?

BESS. I'd like to do what you did.

SHELBY. Marry a stranger?

BESS. No, do something .. pure. There's something about your joy. *(Crosses to her.)* The way you two look at each other, that made me realize that one of the reasons I was so upset with you was that I was jealous. I wanted to be young again .. and in love .. and out of this .. terrible limbo. *(Crosses R.)*

SHELBY. So does Dad.

BESS. *(Sinks into armchair.)* Yes ... but only in Texas!

SHELBY. *(Crosses to R side of sofa, sits.)* Mother, you haven't been listening to him. He doesn't want what's in Texas. He wants you!

BESS. He wants me *there*!

SHELBY. He doesn't care where he has you. He just wants you. He would give up that offer if you would quit the show. I know it! I'm sure of it.

BESS. So we both quit. Then we're both out of jobs. And then what???

SHELBY. I thought this was about love, not about jobs!

BESS. Well it is.. *(Crosses DC to table.)* .. but .. I've worked so hard to be successful.

SHELBY. You've *been* successful. Now be something else.

(Door opens, in bursts LES and DAVID.)

DAVID. Look who got out of the cab!

LES. Hi! *(Puts down overnight bag near railing.)*

SHELBY. Dad! *(Runs UC, embraces LES. BESS goes to sofa, sits, puts newspapers on coffee table. DAVID lingers near bookcase.)*

LES. What did I do to deserve this?

SHELBY. I'm leaving.

LES. What?

SHELBY. I mean, I'm glad you're home, because I wanted to see you before I left.

LES. Where are you going??

SHELBY. With Roger.

LES. Roger? Oh. Right! Roger .... to Utah.

SHELBY. Virginia.

LES. He's from Utah, why are you going to Virginia?

SHELBY. He works in Virginia.

DAVID. He works *out of* Virginia. *(Mimes waves on the ocean.)*

LES. Oh. The ship. Of course. Well! *(Crosses with her, DC.)* Can't you stay a few more days ... so we could celebrate. Take you to dinner. A show. Maybe even just sit and talk.

BESS. I tried. They want to go and get settled there.

LES. Well ... have a wonderful ... uh .. we didn't even get you a wedding present.

SHELBY. *(She kisses him.)* Bye Dad. *(Hugs him again.)*

(ROGER comes in, stands at door.)

ROGER. *(even more exasperated)* Shelby, what's going on?

LES. Roger! *(Crosses U to ROGER, shakes hands. SHELBY crosses to sofa, sits, hugs BESS.)*

ROGER. Yes sir!

LES. Son!

ROGER. Yes sir!

LES. It's strange calling someone son, you've only known two days.

ROGER. Yes sir. Well, goodbye sir. *(Crosses DC to sofa.)*

LES. *(following DC)* Hold it! You can't leave. We have to have a regular wedding celebration.

ROGER. I've got to go on duty, sir. *(Leads SHELBY U to door, but she grabs railing and will not leave.)*

DAVID. *(Crosses DR of sofa.)* Dad .. you started to tell me about Houston. What happened?

LES. Ohhh, it was terrific. Bess, you should have come with me. It was terrific!

BESS. *(Crosses UR, above sofa, and out to kitchen.)* I don't want to hear about Houston! Everybody's leaving! The family's breaking up. I don't want to hear it!

LES. *(follows her out)* David...'s still going to be here.

DAVID. No, actually I'm going to Los Angeles with Jeff Pozner to form a rock and roll band.

LES. *(Comes back in, stands above table.)* A rock and roll band? But you don't know anything about music! *(BESS quickly follows him back in and crosses to CS.)*

DAVID. That's what's great about rock and roll!

LES. What about college?

DAVID. I can always go back to college. Rock and roll may not last much longer.

BESS. Oh God........

ROGER. *(at door, hand on handle)* Shelb? Can we.....

BESS. We are falling apart. We are Falling Apart! *(She begins to cry and runs off to bedrooms thru UR arch.)*

LES. *(after her)* Bess! We aren't falling apart. *(DAVID counters USL.)*

BESS. No! No! — Noooo! — *(exits)* .....we're falling apart! *(LES after her. The door slams.)*

ROGER. *(Slams front door. Pause, then:)* HOLY MOSES! HOL—LY MOSES!

SHELBY. *(at R of door)* Is something wrong, honey?

ROGER. *(totally losing control)* Is something wrong? Is something wrong? That's what's wrong with you people. You don't even know when something's wrong. Don't you ever say anything nice to each other? I've been here three days and I don't think I've heard anyone say anything nice to anyone else. I mean Shelby said her family was "fun." Well, this is not what I call fun!

SHELBY. *(Steps in to him.)* Honey ... just.......

ROGER. What is the matter with you people? Are you all sick or what? *(Crosses DC.)* HOLY MOSES!! Radio programs in the morning. On the air. Off the air. Big parties. Big celebrities. So what? So what?? *(to DAVID)* You know, Shelby is a different person when she's not cooped up in here. She is a different person, thank the good Lord for that. You people are all out of your minds. Just because you got a radio program and you got a column in the paper, does that allow you to run around and scream at each other and bait each other and make the remarks you make about each other. I mean what kind of a family is this anyway?????

DAVID. Roger, my boy. *(Crosses to him, pats his shoulder.)* It's your family now. *(ROGER sinks into C chair at table.)*

LES. *(Enters from bedrooms, crosses to C of railing.)* I think your mother's in some kind of hysterical shock. She ... can't stop crying.

DAVID. *(Crosses to sofa, sits, picks up* Variety.*)* Maybe she's just unhappy. Nothing's going her way.

SHELBY. Da-vid!

LES. Shelb .. maybe you better go in there. She won't take comfort from me. I think the shock of my actually getting this job offer is too much for her. *(SHELBY starts to bedroom, thru UR arch. ROGER rises as if to protest but it's no use. He sits in chair below railing, picks up the book he had left on the credenza and animatedly mutters to himself. LES looks at him and just smiles. He picks up one of the autographed baseballs from the bookcase and crosses D to R of sofa.)*

DAVID. So, when are you taking the job?

LES. I'm going to discuss it with your mother first.

DAVID. *(sighs)* I'm going to the john. *(picking up* Variety*)* Wanna see if there are any apartment listings in L.A. *(reading as he goes toward kitchen)* Jeeze, lookit this. Spanish Villa with two pools for rent. Costs less than this apartment. What do they need *two* pools for??

LES. One to drive into.

DAVID. Right. *(He exits. LES, alone with ROGER, faces DS as ROGER rises and crosses UC just in time to see LES "warming up" to pitch the ball. ROGER pretends to read, just as LES turns to see him.)*

LES. So.

ROGER. So.

LES. *(Steps U to below railing.)* I see you're reading *Anna Karenina.* Like it?

ROGER. I've read it before.

LES. Ah, wonderful book, isn't it?

ROGER. I thought you never finished it.

LES. Well, I like it so far. *(They eye each other awkwardly.)*

(SHELBY bursts in thru the US arch.)

SHELBY. *(Stands above railing.)* Dad! I think you better go back in there. *(LES starts to say, "Why?")* I knocked at the door, but she wouldn't answer.

LES. SO?

SHELBY. Well, God knows what she could be doing in there. Swallowing pills? Slitting her wrists?

LES. Reading *Vogue*!

(DAVID re-enters from kitchen.)

DAVID. Dad! Have you seen the trades?

LES. No.

DAVID. *(crossing to CS)* You've been cancelled.

LES. What??? *(Crosses to CS, next to DAVID as DAVID reads. SHELBY crosses D and joins them standing on LES' R.)*

DAVID. "Robert Steiner, head of programming, and Rupert Dixon, chairman of RKO radio, announced today that all of its remaining talk shows would be cancelled immediately. RKO is undergoing a major re-programming structure to appeal to the younger mass-market audience. Asked..."

LES. *(taking the paper from him and reading the last sentence)* "Asked if that meant rock music, Dixon replied, 'No comment.' " Ha hahaaaaaaa! That's terrific! Does your mother know? Has she read this?!

DAVID. Not that I know of. She didn't say anything.

(ROGER, silently, but with great purpose, exits to the bedroom, USR, unseen by others.)

LES. *(Turns to go.)* I've got to tell her!

SHELBY. *(stopping him)* NO! You can't tell her now. She's too upset to be told. She might do something desperate!

LES. You're mother is not going to do anything desperate. She is a strong woman.

SHELBY. Strong women don't sit alone and cry in bathrooms. She's not a strong woman. She's a weak woman with a strong personality!!! *(DAVID and LES look at each other.)* I'll get her out here. We women understand each other. *(She starts to cross U, gets as far as C railing.)*

(ROGER enters with BESS, from DSR. BESS is walking slowly, in a slight state of shock. They all look ... quite surprised at the entrance.)

SHELBY. Roger????

DAVID. Mom????

LES. Bess...? *(He moves a step forward.)* Roger my boy ... how did you do it?

ROGER. I just told her you were cancelled. She came out pretty quick. *(Crosses U to door, stands and waits.)*

BESS. Les ... is it true...? Is it really true?

LES. *(nods)* It's in *Variety.*

BESS. I know, but is it *true*? *(He gets paper, shows it to her. She sits slowly on sofa and reads.)* There's only one word for those people; Insensitive Brutes! They couldn't have called us? Come over here personally to deliver the news. Noooo. They send it out as a press release. We have to pick up the paper and read it the same time that everybody else is reading it. How humiliating!!!

LES. Bess. What's the difference how we're cancelled. We're *cancelled.*

BESS. The difference is class. They have no class. We've been on the air ten years .. *exuding* class. We *mean* class to millions of Americans .. and those ... those spineless chumps .. haven't got enough class to cancel us like gentlemen. Well, I wouldn't work for them again if they came crawling on their knees! *(She suddenly bursts into uncontrollable tears.)*

LES. *(Crosses to sofa, sits next to BESS, tries to comfort her.)* Come onnn, Bess. Now, it's not the end of the world. Come on.

BESS. No. *(rises)* It's not the end of *your* world. You've got something to do. I've got nothing! *(Crosses R.)*

SHELBY. *(Crosses d, to above end table.)* Mom, you've still got your column. Your TV game show.

BESS. They're not the same. The show is my job. My life. It's what people know me from. Without it, I'll be a nobody.

DAVID. *(at C)* I doubt that.

BESS. You just wait and see. People are fickle. They love you for ten years, they forget you overnight.

SHELBY. But Mom, it's perfect. Now you can go with Dad!

BESS. I don't want to go to Texas! *(She falls to the floor in despair.)* What's in Texas? Les, do you really want to go to Texas???

DAVID. Of course he does. It's the chance of a lifetime. Jesus, Mom!

BESS. *(Sits up, crawls to R end of coffee table.)* Are you taking the job? Les, did you take the job?

LES. Well, it's a terrific job. Back in the old booth again. And they're gonna have *some* organixation down there. Lots of money. They showed all the terrific plans they've got for the future. That's sommmme operation!

DAVID. It's what you've always wanted.

LES. Yes! Ohhh yes. It's terrific all right. Yes.... *(He sighs.)*

BESS. *(sitting on floor)* But....

LES. *(Rises, slowly crosses to L of table, still holding baseball. DAVID counters to his R and sits on the L arm of the sofa, facing LES.)* Well, this is gonna sound strange, but do you know what they're planning to do down there? They're gonna build a stadium with a roof over it! An indoor baseball park. Keep the temperature the same. No rainouts. No heat waves. And get this ... artificial turf. No grass! Nooo grass! They're gonna play baseball on this big green rug! I remember when I was a kid ... going out to the ball park in St. Louis. The ball parks were always in lousy neighborhoods. And you'd go through these crummy streets ... and onto this crummy park .. and suddenly... Wow ... all this grass. It was so green. And there was so much of it. It was one of the wonders of my boyhood. I can't believe they're gonna take that away. And no sun. I mean it'll show through the roof ... but you can't just sit up in the bleachers and ... bake. And no wind! I mean if a player can't lose the ball in the sun or if the wind can't carry a 220 hitter's fly into the stands now and then ... what kind of baseball game is that going to be?

DAVID. What difference will that make with your job?

LES. It's going to change the game! *(Sits at table, L chair.)*

DAVID. Maybe for the better.

LES. I don't call playing baseball indoors, better!

BESS. The theatres used to be outdoors. Moving them inside hasn't seemed to hurt them.

LES. It's not the same.

DAVID. *(Crosses to table, sits on C chair.)* Yes, it *is* the same. It's progress. Dad, give it a chance.

LES. There's some things progress is bad for. Baseball is one of them. Next thing you know they'll be trying to speed up the game. If you speed up the game, it's not baseball.

DAVID. Dad, you cannot turn down this job just because they are going to play indoors. It's the job you've wanted. You can't do this. You can't do this to yourself.

LES. It just doesn't feel right.

DAVID. Give it a chance.

LES. If I give it a chance, I could get stuck there just like I'm stuck here.

BESS. You're not stuck here. *(Rises, crosses to C.)* You can get away any time you want. This job will get you away. *(really meaning it)* Take it. Go ahead. Take it. *(She turns away, teary again. Moves across the room to US, below the desk. LES looks at her, with DAVID, ROGER and SHELBY waiting to see the next move. ROGER, who has been holding a copy of* Anna K. *the whole time, now crosses DR, slams the book down on the credenza and heads for the door.)*

SHELBY. *(Crosses U to him.)* Wait. I wanna see what's going to happen.

ROGER. Fine. You wanna stay. Stay, but if you stay, I can tell you right now what's gonna happen to us.

SHELBY. *(She looks at him, then rushes to her mother, hugs.)* Bye Mom. *(Crosses D to LES.)* Bye Dad. *(She gives DAVID a little smack on the head and crosses U to door.)*

DAVID. Taking a cab?

ROGER. Yes.

DAVID. Give me a lift to school.

SHELBY. We're going to the airport.

DAVID. That's close enough. *(He crosses U and exits, then SHELBY exits. ROGER nods to BESS and salutes LES, who salutes back. ROGER exits, closes door. LES and BESS are alone. She turns and moves to phone at the credenza.)*

LES. What are you doing?

BESS. I'm going to call the station. They can't do this to us.

LES *(He moves to her as she dials and stops her.)* Bess, don't. *(Takes phone from her, hangs it up and crosses back to table.)*

BESS. What are we going to do? Are you going to go?

LES. You know what I'd like to do?

BESS. What?

LES. Make a deal. I'll give up Texas — if you'll give up the show.

BESS. Give it up? It's over. It gave us up!!

LES. Bess, I know you. You'll be on the phone to CBS, NBC and ABC and have us on again tomorrow!

BESS. *(with finality)* Talk shows have had it.

LES. You'll have us playing records. You'll have us on! You get what you want.

BESS. What do you want?

LES. *(He looks at her.)* I want you.

BESS. Les ... I can't take it when you're like that.

LES. What?

BESS. *(Starts to cry.)* Romantic.

LES. I'm not being romantic. I'm being honest.

BESS. That's worse. *(Crosses DR to sofa, lies down.)*

LES. Look ... we've tried *everything.* And you know damn well, we've never reall been happy since we stopped paying attention to each other. I'll make you a deal. I'll give up Texas. You give up New York.

BESS. And where would we go?

LES. I don't know. Connecticut! Yes, Connecticut. We own a home there! We've never lived in it!

BESS. And what do we *do* there?? *(Sits up slowly.)*

LES. I could *write* my book. And you could *write yours.* We could kick the sublets out of the house in Connecticut. We've never lived there. How about that? *(Crosses to sofa, sits next to her.)* We could actually live in our house. We could live there. Together. Work there together. We could even come into New York now and then.

BESS. What about my column?

LES. Give it up! You don't really like writing that crap. You're just used to the income!

BESS. No ... it's fun ... seeing all those people .. going to all those...

LES. You don't get a Pulitzer Prize writing about who's with whom at 21!

BESS. I don't know .. if I can write something good. I was 24. I haven't written anything of substance in years.

LES. How are you going to find out if you don't start?

Starting is the hardest part. Take it from me.

Bess. What are you talking about? Starting's easy for you ... you start hundreds of things. You never *finish* anything.

Les. OK. I'll help you start and you'll help me finish! And we'll write those damn books. And we'll have breakfasts together where we don't *have* to talk. Or we'll sleep thru breakfast. Free people can do that!

Bess. Well ... how about the game show? Once a week? I could come in once a week and do that.

Les. Why?

Bess. *(pouting)* It's fun. I'm the smartest one on the panel. I like to show off!

Les. *(laughs)* Good. You can still do that. Once a week to New York. That sounds good. And I'll come in and drink with the boys at Toots Shors .. and see a ball game or a fight. And then Monday .. back to the sticks!

Bess. Would we keep this apartment?

Les. Is that really important to know now? We'll sublet it to the Dalcimers!

Bess. Oh Less... *(teary)*

Les. What???

Bess. I don't know.

Les. What??

Bess. *Yesterday* we were on the verge of divorce. How can we seriously decide to drop everything *today* and run off and live together. That's crazy!

Les. *(He puts his arm around her.)* I don't know. I think it's a hell of a lot less crazy than indoor baseball. *(She looks at him for a moment, then totally capitulates, putting her arms around him. They hug.)*

(Phone rings. They look at each other, decide to ignore it, snuggle again. It rings again. They ignore it. It rings again. LES covers BESS' ears with his hands. It rings again. He looks at her, picks up the phone and hands it to her.)

BESS. *(into phone)* Yes. What? ... Oh... But ... I .. Yes... OK ... Sure ... OK. *(Hangs up.)*

LES. What?

BESS. *(She runs to the cabinet.)* We're on!! We're on in TWO!!!

LES. Wait a minute. We're cancelled!

BESS. *(Starts setting up the equipment.)* We have two more weeks. They have to give you two weeks notice.

LES. The hell with 'em. The way they told us. In the paper. Forget it!!!

BESS. OH Les, we owe it to our listeners. Let's go gracefully. *(no response from LES)* Two weeks. What's two weeks?

LES. It's going to seem like two milleniums.

BESS. Nooo. Look .. we'll do things we've never done before. We'll have fun!

LES. Yeah, sure.

BESS. *(She sets up mike, picks up studio phone. Into phone.)* Yes. All set... *(into mike)* Good morning. One two three four. *(into studio phone)* OK ... thanks. *(She turns to LES.)* What do *you* want to talk about? We'll talk baseball. Every day. For two weeks. Baseball. OK?

LES. *(Rises and crosses R.)* I don't wanna talk baseball. I wanna call it quits NOW.

BESS. We owe our listeners something.

(Yellow warning light flashes.)

BESS. *(cajoling him)* Two weeks, Les. *(She flicks the monitor switch on and sits on C chair at table.)*

ANNOUNCER. It's 8:05. And time for Breakfast with Les and Bess. With Bess Christen and Les Dischinger. So let's go up to their cozy apartment here in Manhattan and have some breakfast.

(Red "on air" light goes on. BESS switches off monitor. LES crosses to table, passing credenza, and, unseen by BESS, picks up the copy of Anna K.*)*

BESS. *(genuinely)* Good morning, darling.

LES. *(a tense pause as he sits, then:)* Good morning, dear.

BESS. Well, as many of you may or may not know, we are going off the air in two weeks. Actually, we just found out about it, ourselves, this morning, rather unceremoniously .. but such is life. Anyhow .. we thought we'd like to go out with something rather special. Maybe just talk about some of our favorite things. Tell some of our favorite stories.

LES. Right! I'd like to start off with one of *my* favorites. OK? Hon?

BESS. Sure.

LES. *(Produces the book and opens it. BESS is surprised, but then just nods and smiles.)Anna Karenina* by Leo Tolstoy. Chapter one. "Happy families are all alike; every unhappy family is unhappy in its own way. Everything was in confusion in the Oblonsky's household...." *(He continues reading.)*

(As The Curtain Falls)

COSTUME PLOT

BESS: Royal blue or red long-sleeve, floor-length, belted robe in heavy silk or satin with matching high-heel mules

Light-weight floor-length nightgown in powder blue or off-white

Wrist watch, wedding band and other rings

LES: Long-sleeve pajamas in a loud print

Long-sleeve, knee-length striped bathrobe (cotton or silk) with belt

Black leather slippers

White handkerchief

Wedding ring

SHELBY: Shortie pink nightgown with matching 3/4 sleeve robe and baby doll bottoms

Fluffy pink slippers

Pale pink hair ribbon

Wedding ring

ROGER: White boxer shorts

Light blue cotton long-sleeve, knee-length bathrobe with belt

Dog tags, Wedding ring, Wrist watch

112

DAVID: Black tuxedo—distressed, dirty, wrinkled, wet, and too big
Black cumberbund
Very dirty white formal dress-shirt (too big)
Wrist watch

Dark green, long-sleeve sweatshirt
Long-sleeve pink button-down collar shirt
Faded, torn jeans
Black high-top sneakers (no socks)
Wire-rim glasses

ACT II, Scene 1

BESS: Ankle-length strapless black satin gown with gold silk sash—straight skirt, very form-fitting
Floor-length full black satin coat with gold silk lining, elbow-length puffed sleeves and high collar
Long black gloves and matching clutch purse
Black satin high-heel sling-back shoes
Expensive jeweled necklace, earrings and bracelet

LES: Black tuxedo and cumberbund
Black bow tie
Black shoes
White formal dress shirt with studs and cuff links
Black socks
Wrist watch

SHELBY: Spaghetti-strap, knee-length, pink party dress
                with flared skirt
            Pearl necklace
            White high-heel shoes
            Pink hair ribbon

            Hot pink bath towel and pink slippers

DAVID: Gray slacks with belt
            Pale yellow or blue shirt—long sleeves roll-
                ed up
            Tie (small paisley pattern or stripe)
            Brown penny-loafers (no socks)

            Checkered flannel pajamas

ROGER: White U.S. Navy Ensign uniform and hat
            White slip-on shoes
            White T-shirt and socks

            Boxer shorts and bathrobe (same as ACT I)

NATE: Black tuxedo and shoes
            White formal dress shirt with cuff links
            Red plaid cumberbund
            Red plaid bow tie
            Red plaid pocket handkerchief

ACT II, Scene 2

BESS: Long-sleeve men's pajamas, a quiet, simple
    stripe
    Short, silk rose-colored robe with long flared
    sleeves & belt
    Worn-out, old moccasins
    White lace handkerchief

LES: Black and white check or tweed sportscoat
    White shirt
    Gray slacks and black belt
    Striped tie
    Black shoes and socks

SHELBY: Three-piece cotton suit; royal blue straight
    skirt and 3/4 sleeve waist-length jacket, red
    & white polka dot blouse with large tie bow
    Red hair ribbon
    White high-heel shoes

ROGER: Same uniform, etc. as ACT II Scene 1

DAVID: Old green army coat, light-weight, long
    sleeves with a Peace emblem sewn on the
    back
    Same dark green sweatshirt, same jeans,
    same sneakers as ACT I

PROPERTY PLOT

Pre-Set (On Stage):

Pile of newspapers on floor in hall outside front door
       includes: Daily Variety, N.Y. Post, Herald Tribune,
       N.Y. Times. (pre-set for every scene)

Roger's suitcase w/bathrobe inside, on floor at R of door
       (ACT I)

On Desk: (same at the top of every scene)
       Beige telephone, pencil cup w/sharpened pencils,
       nail file, letter opener, practical lamp, ashtray, Bess'
       steno pad, clipboard (with lists attached about com-
       mercial lead-ins and product sponsors), 3 different
       color folders (one with refugee kids letters, one with
       celebrity photos, one with newspaper clippings
       and articles)

On Radio Cabinet: (ACT I)
       Large bouquet of silk flowers in brass container,
       automatic coffee percolator w/brown liquid inside,
       two china cups and saucers, microphone w/plug-in
       cord attached is inside, skeleton-type key is in the
       door of the cabinet

On Dining Table (ACT I)
       Black studio phone (w/attached light) and monitor
       console (w/red and yellow lights), are already
       plugged in to special effects socket on floor under
       table.

Two chairs are at the table, one in the center, one at the left.

On Credenza: (same for every scene)

Beige telephone (practical ring), small wooden file box w/index cards inside, address/date book, a framed photograph, a small bowl of silk flowers, a practical lamp

Inside drawer: more commercials lists and loose sheets of paper

On Coffee Table: (ACT I)

Couple of bric-a-brac items, ie: large conch shell, crystal paper weight, ashtray and two 1961 *Life* magazines

On End Table: (same for every scene)

Two framed photographs on DS end and an ashtray in between them

On Mantle: (same for every scene)

Two ginger jar type vases w/lids on either end, a couple of small plants in brass containers, two autographed baseballs on tiny stands, three trophies of various sizes and a couple of framed photographs

In Fireplace: (same for every scene)

Large brass fan-type screen and slightly US, brass fireplace implements in a stand

In Bookcase: (same for every scene)

Several hardcover volumes of various sizes (some complete sets), almost one entire shelf of *Anna Karenina* books (mostly paperbacks), another autographed baseball on a tiny stand, the stereo receiver (w/practical light in it) and a few small vases and other bric-a-brac

On Sofa:

Four small throw pillows, Ensign's cap (pre-set on SR side, ACT I only)

The Kitchen: (has a visible window w/open curtains)

We can see a double sink, dishtowel rack, paper-towel rack, etc. On the counter there must be: napkin holder w/linen napkins, a can of furniture polish, a dust cloth, extra coffee cup and saucer, bowl w/cornflakes and a spoon, bottle of milk (about 1/2 full).

Inside one of the cabinets: a small white pastry box w/cookies in it and several single-serving boxes of cornflakes.

Other (Optional) Dressing:

Brass magazine holder w/magazines & newspapers DS, next to the large upholstered armchair, large leafy plant-tree behind the chair

A four-shelf brass and glass etergere w/assorted bric-a-brac at the R of the front door and a porcelain umbrella stand w/two umbrellas

The window draperies are expensive and floor-length, pre-set open thru-out the play with a sheer in the middle, covering the window but allowing in the light. The SR window is always left half open.

There is a two-tier glass and brass tea cart on the USL wall, below the kitchen arch w/a plant on the bottom shelf and two 1/2 full crystal decanters, a large brass hour glass and a crystal bud vase on the top shelf.

On the wall SR are four brass electric candleabras (3 frosted bulbs each) which are practical.

The entire set is covered in soft beige carpeting.

Pre-set (Off-Stage Right):
  David's schoolbooks
  3 suitcases & make-up case (II-2)
  Shopping bag w/quilt in it (II-2)
  4 strung clusters of ballons (II-1)
  Cinderella pillow (II-2)
  Small black leather overnight case (Les II-2)
  Silver serving tray (II-1)
  Vacuum cleaner w/long cord (II-1)
  2 cardboard liquor boxes (can also be used as bottle storage) (II-1)
  Note: the quick change area is also off-right)

(Pre-set (Off-Stage Left):
  3 strung ballon clusters & long crepe paper streamers (II-1)
  Several rolls of confetti-type streamers for the railing (II-1)
  2 suitcases
  4 cardboard liquor boxes (more storage-II-1)
  4 large shopping bags (II-1)
  Girl's hat (II-1)
  1 bowl (or wicker basket) of chips (II-1)
  2 bowls (or baskets) of popcorn (II-1)
  4 dozen assorted quart size liquor bottles (II-1)
  Package of 100 paper cups (II-1)
  Masking tape (to hang banner & streamers)

Note On Scene Change Between II-1 And II-2

Room should be restored and suitcases pre-set in less than 45 seconds.

Scene change lights include all on-stage practicals and early-morning sunlight thru the windows.

"Whistle While You Work" theme and another HOST V.O. should play during the change.

PERSONAL PROPS

Bess . . . . set of front door keys
Les. . . . . piece of sheet music w/*Because of You* on it
Nate. . . . . two one-dollar bills